# Zohar

Books in the
# SkyLight Illuminations Series

# Zohar

## Annotated & Explained

Translation & annotation
by Daniel C. Matt

*Foreword by Andrew Harvey*

*Walking Together, Finding the Way*®
SKYLIGHT PATHS®
PUBLISHING
Woodstock, Vermont

# Zohar: Annotated & Explained

2009 Quality Paperback Edition, Fifth Printing
2007 Quality Paperback Edition, Fourth Printing
2005 Quality Paperback Edition, Third Printing
2004 Quality Paperback Edition, Second Printing
2002 Quality Paperback Edition, First Printing
© 2002 by Daniel C. Matt
Foreword © 2002 by Andrew Harvey

The cover art, by Tim Holtz, depicts the ten *sefirot*, the various aspects of divine reality. For an explanation, see "Introduction to the *Zohar*," pp. xxvi–xxix, and the diagram on p. xxii.

Grateful acknowledgment is given for permission to use material from *Zohar: The Book of Enlightenment*, a volume in the Classics of Western Spirituality series, translated and introduced by Daniel Chanan Matt, © 1983. Published by Paulist Press, Mahwah, N.J.; www.paulistpress.com. Used with permission of the publisher.

**Library of Congress Cataloging-in-Publication Data**

Zohar: annotated & explained/translation and annotation by Daniel Chanan Matt.
p. cm.—(SkyLight illuminations)
Includes bibliographical references and index.
ISBN-13: 978-1-893361-51-5 (quality pbk.)
ISBN-10: 1-893361-51-9 (quality pbk.)
1. Zohar. 2. Cabala. 3. Bible. O.T. Pentateuch—Commentaries.
I. Matt, Daniel C. II. Series.
BM525.A59 Z64 2002
296.1'62—dc21
10 9 8 7 6 5                                                    22002004985

SkyLight Paths Publishing is creating a place where people of different spiritual traditions come together for challenge and inspiration, a place where we can help each other understand the mystery that lies at the heart of our existence.

SkyLight Paths sees both believers and seekers as a community that increasingly transcends traditional boundaries of religion and denomination—people wanting to learn from each other, *walking together, finding the way*.

Cover Design: Walter C. Bumford, III
Manufactured in the United States of America

SkyLight Paths, "Walking Together, Finding the Way" and colophon are trademarks of LongHill Partners, Inc., registered in the U.S. Patent and Trademark Office.

*Walking Together, Finding the Way*®
Published by SkyLight Paths Publishing
A Division of LongHill Partners, Inc.
Sunset Farm Offices, Route 4, P.O. Box 237
Woodstock, VT 05091
Tel: (802) 457-4000    Fax: (802) 457-4004
www.skylightpaths.com

For Ana

Isaac embraced faith,

seeing *Shekhinah* dwelling in his wife.

(*Zohar* 1:141a)

בראשית

בריש הורמנותא דמלכא גליף גלופי בטהירו עלאה בוצינא
דקרדינותא בפיק בגו סתים דסתימו מריש ד'אין סוף
קוטרא בגולמא כשין בעזקא לא חוור ולא אוכם לא סומק ולא ירוק ולא גוון כלל
מריד משיח עביד גוונין לאכסר' לגו בנו בוציג'בפיון חד כביעו דמכוס אנטכעא בגוסין
לתתא סתים בגו סתימין מרזא ד'אין סוף בקע ולא בקע אוירא דיליה לא אתיודע
כלל עד דמגו דחיקו דבקיעותיה נהיר נקודה חדא סתימא עלאה בתר הסוא נקודה
לא אתיודע כלל ובגין כך אקרי ראשית מאמר קדמאה דכלא

והמשכילים יזהירו כזהר הרקיע ומצדיקי הרבים כככבים לעולם
ועד זהר סתים דסתימין כטם אוירא דיליה
דמטו ולא מטו בהאי נקודה וכדין אתפשט דסאיר ראשית ועביד ליה
יקרא להיכלוה לתושבחתא' תמן זרע זרעא לאולדא לתועלתא דעלמא ורזא דא זרע
קדם מנכפתא זהר דורע זרע לוקרי'בהאי זרע'דמטי דארגוון טב דאתחפי
לנו ועביד ליה היכלא דאיהו תושבכתא דיליה ותפעלתא דכלא
בהאי ראשית ברא הסוא סתימא דלא אתידע להיכלא דא הוכלא דא אקרי אלהים
ורזא דא כראשי' ברא אלדי' זהר דמכיה כלהו מאחרו אתבדריאו כרוא דאתפשטותא
דנקודה דזהר סתים דא אי בהאי כתב ברא לית תוהסא דכתב מוכרא אלהים
את הסדים בגלמו' זהר דא בראשית קדמאה דכלא אדיר שמיה
קדים גלופ בסטרוי אלדים גלופא בעטרא אסר
סיכלא טמיר גבנו סריאותא דרוז דראשי'ת אסר ראם דכפיק מראשית

# Contents ☐

# Foreword □

## Andrew Harvey

Twenty years ago in Jerusalem—momentarily at peace and flowering in a fragrant and golden spring—I made a friend whose wisdom has sweetened my life; I shall call him "Ezekiel," after one of the wild ecstatic prophets he loved most. He was a wizened, nut-brown, wiry old man in his early eighties with hair so energetic it seemed to dance in white flames on his head. Although his life had seen every kind of suffering and violence (he had been in a concentration camp and fought in the early days for the establishment of a Jewish state before losing all faith in any kind of nationalism), just to be in his presence was to be intoxicated by his passion for God, his unique amalgam of fervor, dry wit and long rich quotations in several languages, and a laugh so wild and loud it sounded, his wife used to say, "like one of the trumpets of the seraphim." We met through mutual friends (who were also friends of the great Scholem, master of modern Jewish mystical studies). They had told me before introducing me, "Now you are ready to meet a real no-holds-barred-kabbalist."

And that is what Ezekiel proved to be. On our very first meeting, after sizing me up and down, asking me pointblank if I knew that the only purpose of life was to know and experience God "like fire in the core of the core of your heart," he grabbed my arm, dragged me into the kitchen, and amidst piles of dishes heaped with salads and whirling delicious smells of borscht and stew, he launched into a wild and fantastical account of the timeless origins of Kabbalah: secret flashes of light

ix

between the Infinite One and the hearts of the angels, Abraham hiding a book in a cave, the four holy letters of the Name of God that "contain the entire truth of all knowledge," and a bewildering succession of prophets and holy sages whose names flashed by me so fast I couldn't remember all of them. He ended by taking my shoulders and saying, "If you want to know more, come to my house tomorrow and we'll take a walk around Jerusalem together and follow the threads of our inspiration from street to street and café to café. You like coffee, don't you?"

In the days that followed—days of holy passion and tenderness that I'll never forget—we strolled together through the winding narrow lanes of old Jerusalem, talking, falling silent, stopping to eat an apple, an orange, or a piece of the Toblerone chocolate he always carried with him in a trouser pocket; halting at tiny, shabby cafés where other old men would hail him, clap him on the back and ply us with cups of coffee. For hour after hour Ezekiel poured out to me a lifetime of distilled knowledge of Kabbalah, pausing, with infinite patience, to explain remarks I did not initially grasp or to unravel in a dazzling dance of commentary and quotations new concepts and ideas that he thought I was ready to try to comprehend. His presence, so focused and fiery and vibrant; his learning, his tremendous poignant simplicity of manner, his gracious, free-hearted hospitality, all fused together to give me a permanent and unforgettable vision not only of the scope of kabbalistic wisdom but of the kind of human being it was intended to engender.

On the third morning we spent together, Ezekiel announced excitedly, "It's another beautiful day; don't let us waste it! Let us go to Safed. You know what Safed means to us kabbalists, don't you? In the sixteenth century, it became the center of kabbalistic learning, the home of such great sages as Moses Cordovero and my favorite of them all, the great Lion, the Ari, Isaac Luria."

He almost pushed me into his small, broken-down jeep and, talking all the way, drove me to Safed, where we walked and walked though narrow lanes perfumed by the fragrance of spring blossoms. The goal of our visit, he gradually explained, was to pray together toward the end of the day in the ancient, dazzlingly white, candelabra-filled synagogue of Isaac Luria himself. Just before we entered it, as we stood in the golden sun-washed courtyard outside, Ezekiel expounded to me Luria's great vision of *tikkun*, the mending of the world through intense soul-work and acts of creative love and justice. "Now," he said, when he had finished, "I think you are ready." I followed him into the pure white radiance of the synagogue. A great, rich peace descended on my whole mind and body. Ezekiel said nothing but gazed at me, smiling with joy. Afterwards, we sat silently watching the first stars burst open in the rapidly darkening sky. Ezekiel began to speak, at first haltingly and quietly, then with gathering majestic clarity.

"We are living," he began, "in a time in which the whole future—not only of Israel but of humanity—is at stake. This is why the wisdom of Kabbalah that was kept hidden for so long, in a closely guarded and protected oral tradition handed down from master to disciple from the time of Moses, is now being written down and given out to anyone sincere and humble enough to try to embody it. Just as the Tibetan mystics kept their wisdom to themselves for almost two thousand years and are now opening its treasures to the world, so we kabbalists understand that the time has come to share what we know. In the pain and struggle of our time, a planetary spiritual civilization is struggling to be born. It will bring together in a way none of us can yet imagine all the highest teachings of all the greatest mystical traditions to give humanity what it needs to meet the terrible challenges it faces and to prepare it for a wholly new and wonderful flowering that the prophecies of many religions foresee. This flowering is not certain, but it is possible if we want it enough and work for it. Sometimes I think of this new spiritual planetary civilization struggling to be born as a vast rose, each of its petals distinct but unified in a larger and radiant order, representing the highest truths of the different traditions. Just imagine, Andrew, what a powerful fragrance it will have! Just to begin to imagine the fragrance of such a rose, the rose for which the whole history of humanity has been a preparation, is to fall silent in wonder and gratitude.

"The glorious tradition of Kabbalah will have a great role to play in the creation and opening of this universal world-rose. The wonderful old man who taught me what little I know used to often say, 'When the world starts to smell the fragrance of the wisdom of the *Ba'al ha-Zohar* ("the author of the *Zohar*"), Moses Cordovero, Isaac Luria, Abraham Abulafia, and the long lineage of Hasidic mystics, even the smallest stones in the dirtiest streets will start to blossom in light!' I think of his certainty often these days, knowing that war will come again. I hope my teacher was right. Would it not be what we need if out of the horror of the twentieth century a new order could arise, like a phoenix, all the more lustrous and magnificent because she has been born from such horror?"

Ezekiel paused, closed his eyes, and seemed to be praying for the inspiration to continue. Then he went on: "There are, I believe, seven interlinked wonders that the tradition of Kabbalah has to offer true seekers everywhere. I think of them as the seven diamonds of a crown of power and revelation that keeps growing and expanding.

"The first wonder that Kabbalah offers is a vision of the Infinite One, *Ein Sof*, as sublime and majestic as anything you can find in the Rig-Veda, or the great Mahayana Buddhist evocations of the Void, or the poetry of Rumi. This vision isn't merely grandly poetic; it is in the highest sense a vision that 'reveals' something of the ineffable mystery of how Creation came to be, one that helps us gaze awestruck into the burning core of the volcano of the Infinite One's power, and listen to the mind-shattering words of the *Ba'al ha-Zohar*, describing the 'beginning' of Creation:

> At the head of potency of the King,
> He engraved engravings in luster on high.
> A spark of impenetrable darkness flashed
> within the concealed of the concealed
> from the head of Infinity..."

1

Ezekiel here paused and wrote out on a piece of paper *Botsina de-Qardinuta*—"a spark of impenetrable darkness"—and then clapped his hands and shouted with joy: "In one brilliant paradox, the *Ba'al ha-Zohar* evokes the Big Bang and goes to the heart of the cosmic dance between matter and anti-matter that modern physicists are only now beginning to begin to understand!"

He calmed down and went on. "The second wonder that the Kabbalah offers is a vision of what I call the Sacred Marriage, the constant fusion of male and female, good and evil, light and dark, through which *Ein Sof* creates and goes on creating the universe. Such a vision of the universe being constantly created and re-created by the opposite powers of the One in a dance of balance is not confined to Jewish mysticism. It is found in ancient Egypt, in the folklore of many tribes, in the Hindu vision of Shiva and Shakti, in the great Taoist unfolding of Yin and Yang. It is worked out, however, with incomparable precision and richness in the works of the greatest kabbalists. For them the secret of 'participating' in the Creation's endless resources of divine energy lies in an evermore profound knowledge of how the 'marriage' of opposites works on every level of the self, consciousness, and matter. Kabbalists believe that no human being can be completely divine, unless, like the original Adam, he or she fuses within himself masculine power and feminine sensitivity on every level of being and in every activity. As the *Ba'al ha-Zohar* writes, 'The blessed Holy One does not place His abode anywhere male and female are not found together.'

"The third wonder of Kabbalah is the open and flowing system of the ten *sefirot*—the divine archetypes—through which the workings of the cosmic Sacred Marriage can be related to and imagined. The ten different *sefirot* represent the various stages of God's inner life as it unfolds in Creation, the dynamics, if you like, of divine personality. They represent at once a tree of life, an androgynous divine body complete with arms, legs, and sexual organs, and the inner spirit-body of the realized human divine androgyne who has, over years of prayer, meditation, and service to others, fused within himself or herself the different 'energies' and 'powers' of God's presence. When you learn to contemplate the sefirot both separately in all their many-tiered significance and then together, you begin to have a clearer and clearer sense of how the Infinite One creates everything that exists and of how each moment is another revelation of one or more facets of *Ein Sof*'s splendors. You come to embody that awareness yourself. As a great kabbalist wrote, 'When you cleave to the *sefirot,* the divine Holy Spirit enters into you, into every every sensation, every movement.'"

Ezekiel paused and took a long sip of red wine, relishing its flavor and rolling it around his mouth.

"The fourth wonder of the crown of Kabbalah—and the clue to the embodiment of divine love and wisdom that I myself love the most, the one through which the other *sefirot* pour their power into this dimension—is *Shekhinah,* the one who dwells. *Shekhinah* is the name given to God's immanence in the Talmud and Midrash. In Kabbalah, however, *Shekhinah* becomes something even greater and more mysterious—nothing less, in fact, than the feminine side of God, daughter of *Binah. Binah* is one of the most sublime of the *sefirot,* manifesting compassion and understanding, and whom kabbalists call 'the Divine Mother'—mother also of *Tif'eret,* the *sefirah* that breathes harmony and divine beauty. For a kabbalist, the goal of the mystical life is to fuse a living love and knowledge of the feminine Divine in all things—*Shekhinah*—with the deepest inner laws of divine beauty and order represented by *Tif'eret*. This fusion, we believe, makes us vessels and agents of divine power and creativity.

"The *Ba'al ha-Zohar* describes how *Shekhinah,* 'the Queen,' went into exile with Israel itself and how the special task of Israel and all individual Jews is to bring about and participate in the reunion between the absolute and *Shekhinah,* the 'king' and the 'queen,' the transcendent 'masculine' and immanent 'feminine,' so that the kingdom of God can at last be born on earth. This vision of the reunion of *Shekhinah*

with the other *sefirot* and *Ein Sof* is not only essential to the Jews however. What will happen to the world if we do not all wake up to nature
as God's glorious body? How will we revere life and do everything we
can to honor and protect it in every way unless we see in all of its man-
ifestations the shining of *Shekhinah*, the radiance of the Mother-Pres-
ence of God?

"If all of us—not just mystics and Jews—are not initiated into the
truth of the motherhood of God, we will destroy the world.

"The fifth wonder of Kabbalah, I believe, is the fertility, inventive-
ness, and creativity of kabbalistic tradition itself. Think of the *Zohar*,
the cornerstone of Kabbalah. It is written in a quirky, polyvalent, poly-
phonic Aramaic; it is at once a commentary on the Torah in a series of
lyrical meditations and visions, and a sort of mystical novel. Its unique
form with its marriage of opposed genres mirrors the greater marriage
that is always taking place in the universe, and is the most exuberant
imaginable celebration of all the varieties of sacred imagination that
make us vulnerable to revelation in all of its forms. In the highest and
finest kabbalist writing and thought, you will always find this dynamic
balance between accepted wisdom and new discovery, reverence for
tradition and brilliant embrace of authentic innovation. Moses Cordovero, drawing on the *Zohar*, called kabbalists 'the reapers of the field.'
'The reapers of the field are the companions, masters of this wisdom,
because *Malkhut*—*Shekhinah*—is called "the apple field" and She
grows sprouts of secrets and new flowerings of Torah. Those who constantly create new interpretations of Torah are harvesting Her.' To put
it in more modern terms: just as physicists tell us, the observer of a sub-
atomic particle transforms reality through the very act of observing; so a
true kabbalist is continually reinventing what he or she is 'receiving'
through the traditions by continual inspired leaps of sacred imagination. The divine liveliness gives all seekers everywhere a wonderful
example of the dance of divine energy in the imagination and of the
transforming fecundity birthed from it.

"The sixth wonder of Kabbalah is a secret that transforms your life when you start to understand it. Let me put this secret bluntly: since God is not just static being but also dynamic becoming, God needs us as we need God.

"We are not here simply to be 'slaves' to the divine will or to vanish into transcendent union with It; we are here to be transparent vessels of Its power and creativity, the healthy and supple limbs, if you like, through which It enacts Its dance in the real. Without our conscious, willed, inspired participation, God is incomplete; God needs us to realize God's design in and for the world. We are co-creators through God's grace with God Itself. What we do and what we choose affects, in fact, not only this world but also the structure of the entire universe. Isaac Luria, expanding on themes already vibrant in the *Zohar,* maintained that when *Ein Sof* contracted to make a 'space' within Itself through which It could emanate Its primordial light to create the Creation, some of the vessels this light passed into 'shattered,' dropping 'holy sparks' that then became imprisoned in matter. The role of the human being and especially of the conscious mystic is to raise these sparks back to origin in two related forms of mending: *tikkun ha-nefesh* (mending of the soul) and *tikkun olam* (mending of the world); in other words, through prayer, contemplation, and acts of holy creativity and justice. When you begin to understand this, a wholly new life stands open!

"We are here to be the 'site' of the Sacred Marriage of heaven and earth, of the primordial light and matter, to be the 'place' where the fusion of all dimensions is effected so that divine passion through us can remake and reshape every arena and institution, every art and science of the world. When all human beings everywhere start to realize both the responsibility and the glorious powers such a relationship to God opens for them, the creation of a new world can begin."

Ezekiel paused and drained the cup of wine in front of him. His eyes wide open and burning with enthusiasm, he ended, "The seventh and crowning wonder of Kabbalah is the participation in the living glory of divine life that those who perform *tikkun* with every aspect of their heart, mind, thought and being can come to experience. The most wonderful account of this participation is the description in the *Zohar* of the wild and holy death—the wedding celebration—of Rabbi Shim'on. His dying is not merely peaceful: it is a divine rapture in which he is given the supreme privilege of revealing to humanity the secret of the universe. Listen with all your heart and mind and soul to what the dying and illumined rabbi says:

> All the days I have been alive, I have yearned to see this day.
> Now my desire is crowned with success.
> This day itself is crowned.
> Now I want to reveal words in the presence of the blessed Holy One;
> all those words adorn my head like a crown...
> I have seen that all those sparks flash from the High Spark,
> hidden of all hidden.
> All are levels of enlightenment.
> In the light of each and every level
> there is revealed what is revealed.
> All those lights are connected:
> this light to that light, that light to this light,
> one shining into the other,
> inseparable, one from the other."

Ezekiel fell silent. Then, leaning forward and softly putting his hands on mine, he said, "The entire universe is a dance of the glory. Pray for me," he said, "that when my death comes—and it won't be long now—some small spark of the glory of Rabbi Shim'on's wedding will illuminate it."

I was too moved to speak. A holy starlit silence spread its shining around us both.

That holy silence radiates throughout my friend Daniel Matt's matchless translation and commentary of these selections from the *Zohar*. Dive headlong into its light silence and allow its power to transfigure you. Each of the *Zohar's* words, Ezekiel told me once, has an angel hovering over it, singing, "Illumine! Illumine!" And who is any of us not to dare to be illumined? As one of the greatest of kabbalists, Abraham Abulafia, wrote:

The purpose of birth is learning.
The purpose of learning is to grasp the Divine.
The purpose of apprehending the Divine
is to maintain the endurance of one who apprehends
with the joy of apprehending.

I would like to dedicate this introduction to my heart-sister Marianne Williamson, as a gift for her birthday, and for the ever-growing truth of her inner and outer work.

# Preface □

I began studying the *Zohar* in 1970 during my junior year abroad at Hebrew University in Jerusalem, its thick volumes simultaneously forbidding and seductive. Deciphering the Aramaic text was a puzzle, a challenge, a quest. Soon I fell in love with the *Zohar,* captivated by its lush imagery and poetic magic.

I returned to Brandeis University, graduated, traveled, and completed a doctorate that focused on the *Zohar.* My dissertation was a critical edition of a fourteenth-century Hebrew manuscript entitled *The Book of Mirrors,* which included the first extended translations of the *Zohar* (from Aramaic to Hebrew).

After receiving my Ph.D., I journeyed to India to escape libraries and footnotes and to taste mysticism. I studied briefly with a guru, practiced yoga and meditation, and toyed with the idea of never returning to the West. But several months later, I felt drawn back, ready to write and teach.

I was invited to compose an annotated translation of selections from the *Zohar* for the Paulist Press, as a volume in their *Classics of Western Spirituality.* I taught Jewish mysticism for many years in Berkeley, California, at the Graduate Theological Union, a school where Jews, Christians, and Buddhists study side by side, stimulating one another.

By the mid-1990s, I thought that I had finished with the *Zohar* itself, and I turned my attention elsewhere. I wrote a book exploring the parallels between Jewish mysticism and contemporary cosmology: *God and the Big Bang: Discovering Harmony between Science and Spirituality* (Jewish Lights). It was liberating to expand beyond the medieval world of ideas and delve into something fresh and modern. I remember one day gazing at the volumes of *Zohar* commentaries on my bookshelves and noticing how dusty they had become. Would I ever peruse them again?

Then, out of the blue, a woman I had never met approached me through a third party, asking if I would agree to compose a new translation of the *Zohar*—not selections, as I had previously done, but a complete annotated translation. She was willing to sponsor me for as long as it took. I was astounded, overwhelmed. For months I wrestled with the proposal, thrilled but aware of the immensity of the task. I tried valiantly to resist, but couldn't.

Now, several years later, having left my professorship in Berkeley, I find myself sitting in the Shalom Hartman Institute in Jerusalem, spending my days engaged with the *Zohar*, working my way slowly but steadily through its dense, luminous texture. The first volumes have begun to appear. The entire work is entitled *The Zohar: Pritzker Edition* (Stanford University Press).

And this book you are holding in your hand? This is a taste of the *Zohar*, drawn from the volume I composed for the Paulist Press but incorporating insights I have gained since then. I have selected the most powerful, uplifting passages and revised the translation. My gifted editor, Alys Yablon Meller, has helped me streamline the annotations for the benefit of anyone venturing into the *Zohar* for the first time.

May this small book inspire and surprise you!

# Introduction to the *Zohar* ☐

*Sefer ha-Zohar,* "The Book of Radiance," has amazed and overwhelmed readers for over seven hundred years, ever since it emerged mysteriously in Spain toward the end of the thirteenth century. The *Zohar* is the masterpiece of Kabbalah, the Jewish mystical tradition.

## What the *Zohar* Is About

The *Zohar* is a commentary on the Torah, the Five Books of Moses, written in the form of a mystical novel. The hero is Rabbi Shim'on son of Yohai, a saint who lived in the second century in the Land of Israel. In the *Zohar,* Rabbi Shim'on and his companions wander through the hills of Galilee discovering and sharing secrets of Torah. On one level, biblical figures such as Abraham and Sarah are the main characters, and the mystical companions interpret their words, actions, and personalities. On a deeper level, the text of the Bible is simply the starting point, a springboard for the imagination. For example, when God commands Abraham, *Lekh lekha* ("Go forth…to the land that I will show you"), the *Zohar* insists on reading the Hebrew words hyperliterally: "Go to yourself," search deep within and thereby discover the divine.[1]

At times, the companions themselves become the main characters, and we read about their dramatic mystical sessions with Rabbi Shim'on or their adventures on the road, including, for example, an encounter with a cantankerous old donkey driver who turns out to be a master of wisdom in disguise.

Ultimately, the plot of the *Zohar* focuses on the ten *sefirot.* (See the chart on p. xxii and a fuller discussion toward the end of this introduction.) The *sefirot* (from a root meaning "to count") represent various stages of God's

# The Ten *Sefirot*

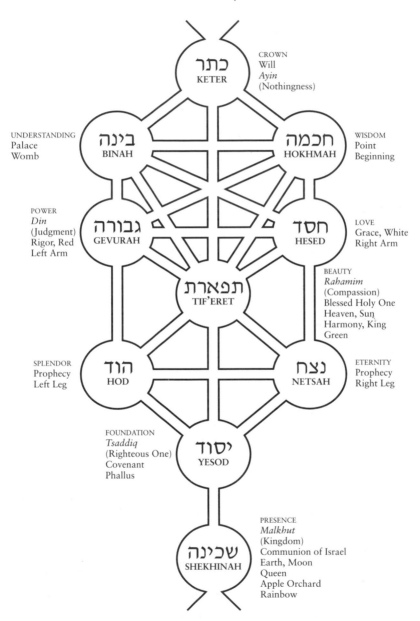

כתר
KETER

CROWN
Will
*Ayin*
(Nothingness)

UNDERSTANDING
Palace
Womb

בינה
BINAH

חכמה
HOKHMAH

WISDOM
Point
Beginning

POWER
*Din*
(Judgment)
Rigor, Red
Left Arm

גבורה
GEVURAH

חסד
HESED

LOVE
Grace, White
Right Arm

תפארת
TIF'ERET

BEAUTY
*Rahamim*
(Compassion)
Blessed Holy One
Heaven, Sun
Harmony, King
Green

SPLENDOR
Prophecy
Left Leg

הוד
HOD

נצח
NETSAH

ETERNITY
Prophecy
Right Leg

FOUNDATION
*Tsaddiq*
(Righteous One)
Covenant
Phallus

יסוד
YESOD

שכינה
SHEKHINAH

PRESENCE
*Malkhut*
(Kingdom)
Communion of Israel
Earth, Moon
Queen
Apple Orchard
Rainbow

inner life, aspects of the divine personality, both feminine and masculine. By penetrating the literal surface of the Torah, the mystical commentators transform the biblical narrative into a biography of God. The entire Torah is read as one continuous divine name, expressing divine being. Even a seemingly insignificant verse can reveal the inner dynamics of the *sefirot*—how God feels, responds, and acts, how She and He (the divine feminine and masculine) relate intimately with each other and with the world.

The *Zohar*'s approach to the Torah is original, often startling. Everyone assumes that the opening chapter of Genesis describes the creation of the world, but for the *Zohar* it alludes to a more primal beginning—the emanation of the *sefirot,* their emergence from the Infinite, known as *Ein Sof* (literally, "Endless").

What are the very first words of the Bible? Everyone knows that: *In the beginning God created....* But for the *Zohar,* which insists on interpreting the original Hebrew words in their precise order, the verse means something radically different: *With beginning, It [Ein Sof] created God* [one of higher *sefirot*].[2] There is a divine reality far beyond our normative conception of "God," and it is this reality that the *Zohar* inspires us to discover and explore.

The immediate reality of God is not foreign to us; it was once our original nature. In the Garden of Eden, human beings were wedded to God. The *Zohar* asks: "Who divorced whom?"[3] The original sin is that we have lost our intimate connection with the divine, our unbounded awareness. Perhaps this loss is an inevitable consequence of tasting the fruit of knowledge, the price we must pay for maturity and culture. The *Zohar* urges us to recover the loss, to regain cosmic consciousness, without renouncing ourselves or the world.

### Who Wrote the *Zohar*?

Based on biblical and rabbinic traditions, the Jewish mystical movement known as Kabbalah emerged in the fertile region of Provence toward the end of the twelfth century. Over the next hundred years, Kabbalah spread over the Pyrenees into Spain. It was here, around the year 1280, that a Spanish kabbalist named Moses de León began circulating booklets. Written in Aramaic, they were peppered with invented words, dense symbolism, and erotic imagery. The tales and teachings were esoteric, yet enchanting. Moses claimed that he was merely the scribe, copying from an ancient book of wisdom. The original had supposedly been composed in the circle of Rabbi Shim'on son of Yohai, a famous disciple of Rabbi Akiva who lived and taught in the second century in the Land of Israel.

These booklets were the first installment of the *Zohar*. De León's claim was widely accepted, and the *Zohar*'s pedigree helped promote the young kabbalistic movement. Few dared to challenge the apparently ancient words of Shim'on bar Yohai and his mystical companions. The book gradually became known as *Ha-Zohar ha-Qadosh*, "The Holy *Zohar*," the canonical text of Kabbalah, and almost all subsequent Kabbalah was based on its teachings.

Only in relatively recent times has Moses de León's actual role been clarified. More than a scribe, De León was the composer of the *Zohar*. He drew on earlier material; he may have collaborated with other kabbalists; and he may have genuinely believed that he was transmitting ancient teachings.[4] In fact, parts of the *Zohar* may have been composed through automatic writing, a technique reportedly used by other kabbalists in which the mystic would meditate on a divine name, enter a trance, and begin to "write whatever came to his hand."[5] But Moses de León wove his various sources into a masterpiece, a book that came to rank with the Bible and the Talmud. Though his name has never appeared on the title page of any edition of the *Zohar*, his bold act of pseudepigraphy transformed Judaism. He must have smiled when he described the *Zohar*'s teachings as "new-ancient words."[6]

### The Language of the *Zohar*

The *Zohar* is written mostly in Aramaic, a language no longer spoken in medieval Spain. The author fashioned this language out of traditional sources he had studied, especially the Babylonian Talmud and the Aramaic translation of the Torah. His unique blend of Aramaic includes strange constructions, grammatical mistakes, and traces of medieval Spanish.

One of the puzzling and endearing features of the *Zohar* is the frequent appearance of neologisms (invented words). The reader often has to guess their meaning or meanings. For example, the newly-coined word *tiqla* can mean "scale, hollow of the hand, fist, potter's wheel, water clock." This last sense refers to a medieval contraption that served as an alarm clock for kabbalists who wanted to be sure to wake up in time for their midnight ritual of studying Torah.[7] (A similar device was used in Christian monasteries so monks could rise for their vigils.) The author of the *Zohar* invented a new word to describe a contemporary invention!

The language of the *Zohar* is poetic, overflowing with multiple connotations. The author writes in such a way that you often cannot pin down the meaning of a phrase. Sometimes an action is stated, then immediately denied: "It split and did not split its aura."[8] Occasionally we encounter oxymorons. One we have just seen: "new-ancient words." Another describes the first impulse of divine emanation: *botsina de-qardinuta*, "a spark of impenetrable darkness."[9] This spark is so bright and powerful that it cannot be seen.

The subject matter of the *Zohar* is mysterious, virtually indescribable, so language can only suggest and hint. Puns, parables, and puzzles abound. The message is not served to you on a platter; you must engage the text and join the search for meaning. The *Zohar* is an adventure, a challenge to the normal workings of consciousness. It dares you to examine your usual ways of making sense, your assumptions about tradition, God, and self.

Through the ages, the potency of the *Zohar*'s language has mesmerized even those who could not plumb its secrets. While kabbalists delved into the mysteries, the unlearned chanted the lyrical Aramaic, often unaware of the literal meaning. In the words of an eighteenth-century mystic, "Even if one does not understand, the language is suited to the soul."[10]

## The Ten *Sefirot*

The essential key to the *Zohar* is the symbolism of the ten *sefirot*, the various aspects of God's personality. Following is a brief outline of this complex spiritual realm. (See the chart on p. xxii.)

The first *sefirah* shares in the unknowability of *Ein Sof* (the Infinite) and is sometimes referred to as *Ayin* (Nothingness). As one kabbalist puts it, "*Ayin* is more existent than all the being of the world. But since it is simple, and every simple thing is complex compared with its simplicity, it is called Nothingness."[11] In this primal state, God is pure, undifferentiated being, neither this nor that, no-thing-ness.

The first *sefirah* is more commonly called *Keter* (Crown). It is the crown on the head of *Adam Qadmon* (Primordial Adam). According to the first chapter of Genesis, the human being is created in the image of God. The *sefirot* constitute the divine archetype of that image, the mythical model of the human being, our original nature. Another depiction of the *sefirot* is a cosmic tree growing downward from its roots above.

Out of the depths of Nothingness shines the primordial point of *Hokhmah* (Wisdom), the second *sefirah*. This point expands into a circle, the *sefirah* of *Binah* (Understanding). *Binah* is the womb, the Divine Mother. Receiving the seed, the point of *Hokhmah*, She conceives the seven lower *sefirot*.

These three highest *sefirot (Keter, Hokhmah,* and *Binah)* represent the head of the divine body and are considered more hidden than the offspring of *Binah*. She gives birth first to *Hesed* (Love) and *Gevurah* (Power), also known as *Din* (Judgment). *Hesed and Gevurah* are the right and left arms of God, two poles of the divine personality: free-flowing love and strict judgment, grace and limitation. For the world to function properly, both are essential. Ideally, a balance is achieved, symbolized by the central *sefirah, Tif'eret* (Beauty), also called *Rahamim* (Compassion). If Judgment is not softened by Love, it lashes out, threatening to destroy life. Here lies the origin of evil, called *Sitra Ahara* (the Other Side).

*Tif'eret is the trunk* of the sefirotic body. He is called Heaven, Sun, King, and the Holy One, blessed be He, the standard rabbinic name for God. He is the son of *Hokhmah* and *Binah*. The next two *sefirot* are *Netsah* (Eternity) and *Hod* (Splendor). They form the right and left legs of the body and are the source of prophecy. *Yesod* (Foundation) is the ninth *sefirah*, representing the phallus, the procreative life force of the cosmos. He is also called *Tsaddiq* (Righteous One), and a verse from Proverbs (10:25) is interpreted as applying to Him: *The righteous one is the foundation of the world*. *Yesod* is the cosmic pillar. The light and power of all the preceding *sefirot* are channeled through Him to the culminating *sefirah*, *Shekhinah* (Presence).

*Shekhinah*, also known as *Malkhut* (Kingdom), is the divine feminine: daughter of *Binah*, bride of *Tif'eret*. She is "the secret of the possible,"[12] receiving the flow of emanation from above and engendering the myriad varieties of life below. The union of *Shekhinah* and *Tif'eret* is the goal of spiritual life. Virtuous human action stimulates *Yesod*, the Righteous One, and brings about the union of the divine couple. Human marriage symbolizes and actualizes divine marriage. Sabbath Eve is the weekly celebration of the cosmic wedding and the ideal time for human lovers to unite.

The mythical imagery of the *sefirot* is stunning. The kabbalists insist that these figures of speech should not be taken literally: they are symbols of a spiritual reality beyond normal consciousness. Sefirotic descriptions are intended to convey something of the beyond. Anyone who becomes fixated on the image itself misses the point.

Critics charge that the theory of *Ein Sof* and the *sefirot* is dualistic, that by describing ten aspects of God, Kabbalah flirts with polytheism. As one kabbalist himself noted, some adherents of the *sefirot* have outdone Catholic adherents of the Trinity, turning God into ten![13] However, the kabbalists maintain that the *sefirot* and *Ein Sof* form a unity, "like a flame joined to a burning coal." "It is they, and they are it." "They are its name, and it is they."[14] From our limited perspective, the *sefirot* appear to possess a multiple and independent existence. Ultimately, however, all of them are one; the true reality is the Infinite.[15] Nevertheless, the prominent mythological character of the system cannot be denied. In a sense, Kabbalah represents "the revenge of myth," resurfacing after being attacked for centuries and being pronounced dead by the medieval philosophers.[16] The kabbalists appreciate the profound nature of myth and its tenacious appeal.

From above to below, the *sefirot* depict the drama of emanation, the transition from *Ein Sof* to Creation. In the words of one early kabbalist, "They constitute the process by which all things come into being and pass away."[17] From below to above, the *sefirot* constitute a ladder of ascent back to the One. The union of the divine couple, *Tif'eret* and *Shekhinah*, engenders the human soul, and the mystical journey begins with the awareness of this spiritual fact of life. *Shekhinah* is the opening to the divine: "One who enters must enter through this gate."[18] Once inside, the *sefirot* are no longer an abstract theological system; they become a map of consciousness. The mystic climbs and probes, discovering dimensions of being. Spiritual and psychological wholeness is achieved by meditating on the qualities of each *sefirah*, by imitating and integrating the attributes of God. "When you cleave to the *sefirot*, the divine holy spirit enters into you, into every sensation and every movement."[19] But the path is not easy. Divine will can be harsh: Abraham, for example, was commanded to sacrifice Isaac in order to balance love with rigor.[20] From the Other Side, demonic forces threaten and seduce. Contemplatively and psychologically, evil must be encountered, not evaded. By knowing and understanding the dark underside of wisdom, the spiritual seeker is refined.

Near the top of the sefirotic ladder, meditation reaches *Binah*. She is called *Teshuvah* (Return). The ego returns to the womb of being. *Binah* cannot be held in thought. She is called Who, implying the meditative question "Who am I?" Such questioning yields nothing that can be grasped, but rather, an intuitive flash illuminating and disappearing, as sunbeams play on the surface of water.[21]

In the depths of *Binah* lies *Hokhmah* (Wisdom). The mystic is nourished from this sphere. Profound and primal, it cannot be known consciously, only absorbed. In the words of Isaac the Blind, one of the earliest kabbalists, "The inner, subtle essences can be contemplated only by sucking, not by knowing."[22] Beyond *Hokhmah* lies the Nothingness of *Keter,* the annihilation of thought. In this ultimate *sefirah* human consciousness expands, dissolves into Infinity.

Only rarely does the *Zohar* explicitly discuss meditation or mystical experience. It focuses instead on the interplay of the *sefirot* and on human conduct. Ethical and spiritual behavior unites the *sefirot,* ensuring a flow of blessing and emanation to the lower worlds; unethical or evil human activity disrupts the union above, empowering demonic forces. The point is that divine and human realms are interdependent. Tradition has always taught us that we need God; the innovative message of the *Zohar* is that in order to manifest in the world, God needs us.

# About the Translation and Annotation □

All translation is inherently inadequate. In the words of the Talmudic sage Rabbi Yehudah, "One who translates a verse literally is a liar; one who adds to it is a blasphemer."[1] To make things worse, the *Zohar* is probably the single most difficult Jewish classic to translate. As I have mentioned, it was composed mostly in Aramaic, yet centuries after Aramaic ceased to be a spoken language. Its cryptic style, puns, and neologisms challenge any reader or translator.

No doubt it is risky to translate the *Zohar,* but it would be worse to leave these gems of wisdom hidden in their ancient Aramaic vault. So I have forged ahead, trying to convey the lyrical flavor of the *Zohar's* poetic prose. Most previous translations smoothed away the roughness of the original Aramaic. I seek to preserve the *Zohar's* ambiguity and obscurity, while making the text accessible.

A typical phrase or passage in the *Zohar* is often not limited to just one meaning. The sensitive reader will ponder various possibilities. In the annotations on facing pages I offer some guidance, explaining the symbolism and identifying rabbinic and kabbalistic parallels. To find the source of a quote in the annotations, see the notes at the back of the book, which are keyed to each *Zohar* passage and annotation number. The glossary identifies the various *sefirot* and other technical terms. The annotated list of suggested readings may stimulate further exploration.

In rendering the selections from the *Zohar* into English, I have at times omitted material. I have taken the liberty of not indicating these omissions with ellipses (...) so as not to interrupt the flow of the translation. Precise citations are provided in the "Index of *Zohar* Passages" at the back of the book so that interested readers can refer to the original.

xxxii **About the Translation and Annotation**

When speaking about God, it is increasingly common to employ inclusive language and avoid the generic use of masculine pronouns. However, to apply this principle invariably to the *Zohar* would violate its nature. Readers soon discover that for the *Zohar*, God is both He and She. The goal is to unite the two, but until the moment of union, the distinct gender of each divine quality should be respected and preserved.

The teachings of the *Zohar* are profound and intense. One who hopes to enter and emerge in peace must be careful, persevering, and receptive. Follow the words to what lies beyond and within. Open the gates of imagination.

# Notes to the Introduction to the *Zohar* ☐

## Introduction to the *Zohar*

1. *Zohar* 1:78a. See Matt, *The Essential Kabbalah*, 127.
2. See chapter 3.
3. See chapter 5.
4. On the composition of the *Zohar*, see Scholem, *Major Trends in Jewish Mysticism*, 156–204; Tishby and Lachower, *The Wisdom of the Zohar*, 1:13–96; Matt, *Zohar: The Book of Enlightenment*, 3–10, 25–32; Liebes, *Studies in the Zohar*, 85–138.
5. See Matt, *Zohar: The Book of Enlightenment*, 27–28.
6. See Matt, "New-Ancient Words: The Aura of Secrecy in the *Zohar*."
7. See *Zohar* 1:92b.
8. See chapter 3.
9. Ibid.
10. Moses Hayyim Luzzatto, cited by Tishby and Lachower, *Wisdom of the Zohar*, 1:29.
11. David ben Abraham ha-Lavan, *Masoret ha-Berit*. See Matt, *Essential Kabbalah*, 66.
12. See David ben Judah he-Hasid, *The Book of Mirrors: Sefer Mar'ot ha-Tsove'ot*, ed. Daniel C. Matt (Chico, Calif.: Scholars Press, 1982), introduction, 29.
13. See Matt, *Zohar: The Book of Enlightenment*, 20.
14. See *Sefer Yetsirah* 1:7; *Zohar* 3:70a, 11b.
15. See chapter 17.
16. See Scholem, *Major Trends in Jewish Mysticism*, 35.
17. Azriel of Gerona, "Commentary on the Ten *Sefirot*." See Matt, *Essential Kabbalah*, 29.
18. *Zohar* 1:7b.
19. Joseph ben Hayyim. See Moshe Idel, *Kabbalah: New Perspectives*, 350, n. 333.
20. See chapter 8.

21. Moses de León, "Commentary on the *Sefirot.*" See Matt, *Essential Kabbalah*, 114.
22. Isaac the Blind, "Commentary on *Sefer Yetsirah.*" See Matt, *Essential Kabbalah*, 113.

## About the Translation and Annotation

1. Babylonian Talmud, *Qiddushin* 49a.

# Zohar

**1** Because of that view…: The man from the mountains claims to be a master of wheat, a master of Torah (the Five Books of Moses). Traditionally, "master of wheat" means one who has mastered the oral tradition. In this parable, wheat and its products (kernels, bread, cake, and pastry) symbolize four levels of meaning in Torah: simple, homiletical, allegorical, and mystical.

The mountain man assumes that because he understands the simplest, literal meaning of the Torah, he has achieved the essence and hence does not need to delve deeper. Although the essence is often the goal of mysticism, this parable implies that essence is inadequate unless it leads to the exploration of deeper levels of meaning inherent in every word.

# 1 □ The Essence of Torah

A parable:

There was a man who lived in the mountains. He knew nothing about those who lived in the city. He sowed wheat and ate the kernels raw.

One day he entered the city. They brought him good bread. He said, "What is this for?"

They said, "Bread, to eat!"

He ate, and it tasted very good. He said, "What is it made of?"

They said, "Wheat."

Later they brought him cakes kneaded in oil. He tasted them and said, "What are these made of?"

They said, "Wheat."

Finally they brought him royal pastry made with honey and oil. He said, "And what are these made of?"

They said, "Wheat."

He said, "I am the master of all of these, for I eat the essence of all of these: wheat!"

Because of that view, he knew nothing of the delights of the world; they were lost to him. So it is with one who grasps the principle and does not know all those delectable delights deriving, diverging from that principle.[1]

1 Sublime secrets: A basic principle of the *Zohar* is that every word in the Torah contains numerous secret meanings, on various levels.

2 *He makes His angels spirits:* This verse is usually understood to mean: "He makes winds His messengers," but Rabbi Shim'on reads it differently.

3 The garment of this world: The angels appear as physical human beings.

4 Torah, who created them…: According to the Mishnah, the Torah itself was the "precious instrument by which the world was created."

## 2 □ How to Look at Torah

*The Torah is full of secrets if only we had many ways of learning their meaning*

Rabbi Shim'on said,
"Woe to the human being who says
that Torah presents mere stories and ordinary words!
If so, we could compose a Torah right now with ordinary words,
and better than all of them!
To present matters of the world?
Even rulers of the world possess words more sublime.
If so, let us follow them and make a Torah out of them.
Ah, but all the words of Torah are sublime words, sublime secrets![1]

"Come and see:
The world above and the world below are perfectly balanced:
Israel below, the angels above.
Of the angels is written: *He makes His angels spirits* (Psalm 104:4).[2]
But when they descend they put on the garment of this world.[3]
If they did not put on a garment befitting this world,
they could not endure in this world
and the world could not endure them.

"If this is so with angels, how much more so with Torah,
who created them and all the worlds,[4]
and for whose sake they all exist.
In descending to this world,
if she did not put on garments of this world,
the world could not endure.

5

**5** Embodiment of Torah: The essential teachings, in this case the commandments, of the Written Torah.

**6** Stories of this world: Various commandments of the Torah are clothed and conveyed in story.

**7** Do not look at the garment...: Those who look not at the garment, but at the body beneath the garment, penetrate the narrative layer and appreciate the commandments of the Torah.

**8** Mount Sinai...: According to the Midrash, the souls of all those who were not yet born were present at Mount Sinai when God revealed the Torah. Here, the *Zohar* suggests that only mystical souls were present, and therefore only they are able to see through the physical layers of the Torah. To be a mystic is to remember the primordial revelation.

"So this story of Torah is the garment of Torah.
Whoever thinks that the garment is the real Torah
and not something else—may his spirit deflate!
He will have no share in the world that is coming.
That is why David said:
'Open my eyes, so I can see wonders out of Your Torah' (Psalm 119:18),
what is under the garment of Torah!

*(handwritten margin note: We have to look beyond the words to understand)*

"Come and see: There is a garment visible to all.
When those fools see someone in a good-looking garment
they look no further.
But the essence of the garment is the body;
the essence of the body is the soul!

"So it is with Torah.
She has a body: the commandments of Torah,
called 'embodiment of Torah.'[5]
This body is clothed in garments: stories of this world.[6]
Fools of the world look only at that garment, the story of Torah;
they know nothing more.
They do not look at what is under that garment.
Those who know more do not look at the garment,
but rather at the body under that garment.[7]
Wise ones, servants of the King on high,
those who stood at Mount Sinai,
look only at the soul, root of all, real Torah![8]
In the time to come they are destined to look
at the soul of the soul of Torah!

"Come and see: So it is above.
There is garment, body, soul, and soul of soul.
The heavens and their host are the garment.
The Assembly of Israel is the body,

9 | Assembly of Israel… Beauty of Israel: In rabbinic literature, *Keneset Yisra'el* (Assembly of Israel) refers to the Jewish people, while in the *Zohar,* it is often associated with *Shekhinah,* the feminine Divine Presence, which is the counterpart of the people, that aspect of God most intimately connected to them. Here *Shekhinah* is described as a body clothed by the heavens, receiving the soul, the masculine aspect of God, which is called *Tif'eret Yisra'el* (Beauty of Israel).

10 | So She is the body of the soul: This is not simply redundant. Rabbinic literature describes a cosmic body containing all souls. In Kabbalah this body is identified with *Shekhinah.* By receiving the soul of *Tif'eret,* She carries all human souls, which are engendered by the union of these two *sefirot.* (See "Introduction to the *Zohar*" for an explanation of the *sefirot,* and the chart on p. xxii.)

11 | The Holy Ancient One: The primal manifestation of *Ein Sof,* the Infinite.

who receives the soul, Beauty of Israel.[9]
So She is the body of the soul.[10]
The soul we have mentioned is Beauty of Israel, real Torah.
The soul of the soul is the Holy Ancient One.[11]
All is connected, this one to that one.   *Ein Sof*

"Woe to the wicked who say that Torah is merely a story!
They look at this garment and no further.
Happy are the righteous who look at Torah properly!
As wine must sit in a jar, so Torah must sit in this garment.
So look only at what is under the garment.
All those words, all those stories are garments."

1 King: God, the Infinite *(Ein Sof)*.

2 A spark of impenetrable darkness flashed: This selection unfolds the meaning of the opening line of Genesis and begins with an oxymoronic description of the first impulse of emanation from the Infinite, initiating the process of Creation. The spark is so bright and powerful that it cannot be seen.

3 A ring: *Keter,* the Crown, the first *sefirah.*

4 Not white, not black…: The vapor within the ring, or crown, was not yet white, black, red, or green (four colors corresponding to the *sefirot* of *Hesed, Shekhinah, Gevurah,* and *Tif'eret*), but a cord mapping out the stages of emanation, the eventual spectrum of divine colors.

5 *Ein Sof:* The Infinite.

6 It split and did not split its aura: This breakthrough of energy, beyond human comprehension, is also beyond description. Therefore the *Zohar* both states and denies the act in one sentence.

7 *Beginning:* The *beginning* mentioned in the first line of Genesis is a point of divine light, appearing as the second *sefirah: Hokhmah* (Wisdom). The point is called *Beginning* because it is the first aspect of God that can be known.

8 First command of all: According to the Mishnah, "The world was created through ten commands." Only nine explicit commands appear in the first chapter of Genesis, but the decade is completed by counting the phrase *In the beginning.*

# 3 □ The Creation of God

*In the beginning*
—GENESIS 1:1

*Ein Sof*

At the head of potency of the King,[1]
He engraved engravings in luster on high.
A spark of impenetrable darkness flashed[2]
within the concealed of the concealed
from the head of Infinity,
a cluster of vapor forming in formlessness, thrust in a ring,[3]   *Keter*
not white, not black, not red, not green, no color at all.
As a cord surveyed, it yielded radiant colors.[4]
Deep within the spark gushed a flow, splaying colors below,
concealed within the concealed of the mystery of *Ein Sof*.[5]
It split and did not split its aura,[6]
was not known at all
until, under the impact of splitting,
a single, concealed, supernal point shone.
Beyond that point, nothing is known,
so it is called *Beginning*,[7] first command of all.[8]

11

**9** *The* zohar *of the sky:* In this biblical verse, the word *zohar* means "radiance, splendor, brilliance." Here it also alludes to the hidden power of emanation and the title of the book.

**10** Then this *beginning* expanded…: The purpose of Creation, according to this interpretation, is to display the glory of the hidden God, which is achieved through a rhythm of revelation and concealment. As the point of light expands, it creates a palace, corresponding to the third *sefirah: Binah* (Understanding). *Binah* is the divine womb, sown by *Hokhmah,* the "seed of holiness." *Binah* then gives birth to the seven lower *sefirot,* which in turn engender the rest of Creation.

**11** Like the seed of fine purple silk…: As a silkworm spins a cocoon out of its own essence, so *Hokhmah,* the point of Beginning, expands into the palace of *Binah.*

**12** God: Hebrew, *Elohim.* Here the name signifies *Binah,* the Divine Mother.

**13** The secret is…: This is the *Zohar's* unique rendering of the opening words of the Bible, which are usually translated: "In the beginning God created." Here the first word, *Be-Reshit,* is translated "With beginning," since the Hebrew preposition *be* means "with" as well as "in." Then the words are read in the exact order in which they appear in the Hebrew, thereby transforming God from the subject of the sentence into its object! This in turn erases the subject, which bolsters the *Zohar's* interpretation that the true subject of divine emanation cannot be named. For the *Zohar,* therefore, the opening words of Genesis mean: "With beginning, the ineffable source created God."

*Those who understand*
*and look beyond the words*
*will be radiant in*
*the sky*

*The enlightened will shine like the* zohar *of the sky,*[9]
*and those who lead many to righteousness, too,*
*like the stars forever and ever* (Daniel 12:3).

*Zohar!* Concealed of concealed struck its aura,
which touched and did not touch this point.
Then this ~~beginning~~ expanded,
building itself a palace worthy of glorious praise.
There it sowed seed to give birth, availing worlds.[10]

*Zohar!* Sowing seed for its glory,
like the seed of fine purple silk
wrapping itself within, weaving itself a palace,[11]
constituting its praise, availing all.

With this *beginning*
the unknown concealed one created the palace.
This palace is called God.[12]
The secret is: *With beginning,* ——— *created God* (Genesis 1:1).[13]

**1** Reserved for the righteous…: This notion is based on the Midrash: "With the light created by God on the first day, Adam could gaze and see from one end of the universe to the other. Since God foresaw the corrupt deeds of the generation of Enosh and the generation of the Flood, He hid the light from them. Where did He hide it? In the Garden of Eden for the righteous, as is written: *Light is sown for the righteous.*"

# 4 □ The Hidden Light

*God said, "Let there be light!" and there was light.*
*God saw how good the light was*
*and God separated the light from the darkness.*

—GENESIS 1:3–4

Rabbi Yitshak said,
"The light created by God in the act of Creation
flared from one end of the universe to the other
and was hidden away,
reserved for the righteous in the world that is coming,
as is written:
*Light is sown for the righteous* (Psalm 97:11).[1]
Then the worlds will be fragrant, and all will be one.
But until the world that is coming arrives,
it is stored and hidden away."

Rabbi Yehudah responded,
"If the light were completely hidden,
the world would not exist for even a moment!
Rather, it is hidden and sown like a seed,
giving birth to seeds and fruit.
Thereby the world is sustained.
Every single day, a ray of that light shines into the world,
animating everything;
with that ray God feeds the world.
And everywhere that Torah is studied at night,

15

**2** Those absorbed in her: In the Talmud, Resh Lakish explains that whoever studies Torah at night is extended "a thread-thin ray of love" during the day. The Ba'al Shem Tov, the founder of Hasidism, explains that the light of Creation is hidden within the Torah, and so whoever studies Torah can see from one end of the world to the other.

**3** Renewing each day…: This parallels the expression in the morning prayer: "Lord of wonders, who renews in His goodness every day continually the act of Creation."

one thread-thin ray appears from that hidden light
and flows down upon those absorbed in her.[2]
Since the first day, the light has never been fully revealed,
but it is vital to the world,
renewing each day the act of Creation."[3]

**1** YHVH Elohim: These are two of the names of God. *YHVH* is the Tetragrammaton, the ineffable name. *Elohim* literally means "God" or "gods" in Hebrew.

**2** Et *Adam:* Grammatically, the word *et* is an accusative particle. It has no independent meaning and is lost in translation, but in rabbinic tradition it often amplifies the original meaning of a biblical verse. Here this word inspires Rabbi El'azar to create a mystical midrash that hints at the true nature of Adam's sin.

**3** If the blessed Holy One divorced Adam: Some commentators have interpreted the Hebrew word *va-yegaresh,* "He drove out," as related to *geirushin,* "divorce," implying that Adam was divorced by God like a wife who has committed an indecent act.

**4** *Et,* precisely!: *Et* (spelled with the two Hebrew letters *alef* and *tav*) is also the Zohar's code name for *Shekhinah,* who symbolizes divine speech: the entire alphabet from *alef* to *tav. Once Et* was driven out of the Garden, language itself became corrupt and remained so until the Revelation of Torah at Sinai. (See the New Testament parallel: "I am *alpha* and *omega.*")

**5** *Adam* actually drove out *Et!:* The nature of Adam's sin is a tightly guarded secret. Here the *Zohar* suggests that his sin was driving out *Et* (*Shekhinah*). He does this by partaking solely of the Tree of Knowledge of Good and Evil (also a symbol of *Shekhinah*), thus separating Her from the other *sefirot* and divorcing Her from Her husband, *Tif'eret* (the Tree of Life). Further, he disrupts the divine-human connection by casting out *Shekhinah* and losing awareness of God's presence. On a psychological level, he separates consciousness from the unconscious.

# 5 □ Adam's Sin

*YHVH Elohim*[1] *expelled him from the Garden of Eden....*
*He drove out* et *Adam*

—GENESIS 3:23–24[2]

Rabbi El'azar said,
"We do not know who divorced whom,
if the blessed Holy One divorced Adam[3]
or not.
But the word is transposed:
*He drove out Et.*
*Et*, precisely![4]
Who drove out *Et*?
Adam.
Adam *actually drove out Et*?[5]
Consequently it is written:
*YHVH Elohim expelled him from the Garden of Eden.*
Why did He expel him?
Because Adam drove out *Et*."

Adam drove out Shekhinah

**1** Making known the Glory on high…: The human being mirrors the structure of the divine realm, the ten *sefirot,* in which masculine and feminine are balanced. The *sefirot* constitute the mystery of faith, the belief system of Kabbalah.

# 6 □ Male and Female

*On the day that God created Adam,*
*in the likeness of God He created him;*
*male and female He created them.*
*He blessed them and called their name Adam*
*on the day they were created.*

Rabbi Shim'on said,
"Supernal mysteries are revealed in these two verses.
*Male and female He created them,*
making known the Glory on high,     *Masculine and feminine*
mystery of faith.[1]                 *are balanced*
Out of this mystery, Adam was created.

*"Male and female He created them.*
From here we learn:
Any image not embracing male and female
is not a supernal, true image.
Come and see:
The blessed Holy One does not place His abode
anywhere male and female are not found together.

21

**2**   Blessings are found only…: In the Talmud Rabbi Hanilai says, "Any man who does not have a wife is without joy, without blessing, without goodness."

**3**   When male and female are as one: This too is based on a talmudic statement: "Rabbi El'azar said, 'Any man [*adam*] who does not have a wife is not an *adam*, as is said: *Male and female He created them…and He called their name Adam.*' " Rabbi Shim'on is also alluding to the original androgynous nature of Adam. According to the Midrash, Adam was created as a male-female entity and was then split into two. Similarly, the divine realm is androgynous, comprising *Tif'eret* and *Shekhinah.* From the union of this divine couple, all souls are born, and these souls too, in their original nature, are androgynous. Only because of Adam's sin, our androgynous nature has been lost. Any man or woman who remains single is only "half a body," but by joining together and engendering new life, each couple extends the chain of being. The inner purpose of human sexuality is to regain wholeness and manifest the oneness of God.

Blessings are found only where male and female are found,[2]
as is written:
*He blessed them and called their name Adam*
*on the day they were created.*
It is not written:
*He blessed him and called his name Adam.*
A human being is only called Adam
when male and female are as one."[3]

1 *He [Abraham] was sitting…Sarah heard…*: This excerpt from Genesis tells the story of three angels coming to visit Abraham in order to tell him that Sarah will conceive and bear a son, although she is already ninety years old and barren. Sarah overhears this prophecy from the tent.

2 *Blessed be the glory of* YHVH *from His place!:* Wherever He is. This understanding of the verse derives from the Talmud: "Behold it is written: *Blessed be the glory of* YHVH *from His place!,* implying that no one knows His place."

# 7 □ Openings

*He [Abraham] was sitting in the opening of the tent. . . .*
*Sarah heard the opening of the tent.*
—GENESIS 18:1, 10[1]

Rabbi Yehudah opened,
*"Her husband is known in the gates*
*as he sits among the elders of the land* (Proverbs 31:23).
Come and see:
The blessed Holy One has ascended in glory.
He is hidden, concealed in utmost loftiness.
There is no one in the world—
nor since the day the world was created has there ever been—
who can comprehend His wisdom or apprehend Him,
for He is hidden, concealed, transcendent, beyond, beyond.

"All beings above and below cannot grasp,
till finally they declare:
*Blessed be the glory of YHVH from His place!* (Ezekiel 3:12).
Those below proclaim that He is above,
as is written: *Your glory is above the heavens* (Psalm 113:4).
Those above proclaim that He is below,
as is written: *Your glory is over all the earth* (Psalm 57:12).
Finally all of them, above and below, declare:
*Blessed be the glory of YHVH from His place!*[2]
For He is unknowable;
no one has ever been able to comprehend Him.
*Yet you say: Her husband is known in the gates?*

25

**3** But indeed, *Her husband is known...*: The passage from Proverbs describing the "woman of valor" is understood to be a hymn to *Shekhinah*, who is married to *Tif'eret*, the blessed Holy One, a more transcendent *sefirah*.

**4** Gates of imagination: Imagination enables the human mind to fathom God, though, as Rabbi Yehudah goes on to say, all imaginative representations fall short of true divine being.

**5** Through these gates, supernal rungs...: Through the *sefirot*, the Unknown becomes known.

**6** He is soul of soul: The human soul originates in God, so He is the essence of this essence. The phrase derives from the medieval Spanish Jewish poet Solomon ibn Gabirol: "You are alive but not through...soul, for You are soul of soul."

**7** Openings for soul: The *sefirot* are openings for the human soul to approach the hidden God, and openings for "soul of soul" to manifest.

**8** *Opening of the tent* is opening of Righteousness...: *Shekhinah* is the opening of the divine realm and is known as Righteousness.

"But indeed, *Her husband is known in the gates*—the blessed Holy One,[3]
who is known and grasped
to the degree that each one opens the gates of imagination,[4]
according to the capacity to attain the spirit of wisdom.
As one fathoms in his mind, so He is known in his mind.
So He *is known in* those *gates*.
But·that He be known accurately?
No one has ever been able to grasp and know Him."

Rabbi Shim'on said,
"*Her husband is known in the gates.*
Who are *the gates*?
As is said: *Lift up your heads, O gates!*
*Be lifted up, openings of eternity!* (Psalm 24:7).
Through these gates, supernal rungs,
the blessed Holy One becomes known,[5]
otherwise no one could grasp.

"Come and see:
The human soul is unknowable
except through limbs of the body,
rungs carrying out what the soul designs.
So she is known and unknown.

"Similarly the blessed Holy One is known and unknown,
for He is soul of soul,[6] spirit of spirit,
hidden and concealed from all,
but through those gates, openings for soul,[7]
the blessed Holy One becomes known.

"Come and see: There is opening within opening, rung upon rung,
through which the glory of the blessed Holy One becomes known.
*Opening of the tent* is opening of Righteousness,
as is said: *Open for me gates of righteousness* (Psalm 118:19).[8]

**9** Now, when this opening is unknown, since Israel is in exile…: Israel's exile symbolizes cosmic dysfunction, the rupturing of sefirotic unity. The higher openings have closed shut and vanished, leaving *Shekhinah* Herself in exile: abandoned by the higher *sefirot* and unknown on earth.

**10** They cannot know or grasp: Israel cannot know.

**11** A *spirit of wisdom and understanding…*: The various spirits in the verse represent higher *sefirot.*

**12** So when Abraham was gladdened: With the news that Sarah would bear a son.

**13** He said—who it was is not recorded. It was *opening of the tent*: The anonymous subject is none other than *Shekhinah.*

**14** Sarah heard the opening of the tent: Noticing the lack of a preposition in the original Hebrew text before the words *the opening*, Rabbi Shim'on interprets this line not as "Sarah was listening at the opening of the tent," but "Sarah heard the Opening of the Tent." She heard *Shekhinah, the opening of the divine* realm, who was revealing the prophecy to Abraham.

This is the first opening to enter;
through this opening all other supernal openings come into view.
Whoever attains this attains all other openings,
for all abide here.

"Now, when this opening is unknown, since Israel is in exile,
all those openings have withdrawn from it;[9]
they cannot know or grasp.[10]
But when Israel comes forth from exile,
all those supernal rungs are destined to alight upon it fittingly.
Then the inhabitants of the world will discover precious, supernal wisdom,
previously unknown to them, as is written:
*The spirit of* YHVH *will alight upon him:*
*a spirit of wisdom and understanding,*
*a spirit of counsel and power,*
*a spirit of knowledge and awe of* YHVH (Isaiah 11:2).[11]
All those are destined to alight upon this lower opening,
*opening of the tent.*
All those are destined to alight upon King Messiah,
so he may judge the world, as is written:
*He will judge the poor with righteousness* (Isaiah 11:4).

"So when Abraham was gladdened,[12] it was by this rung,
as has been said, for it is written:
*He said, 'I will surely return to you when life is due'* (Genesis 18:10).
*He said*—who it was is not recorded.
It was *opening of the tent.*[13]
So *Sarah heard* (Genesis 18:10) this rung speaking,
which she had never heard before,
as is written: *Sarah heard the opening of the tent,*[14]
who was delivering the joyous news:
*'I will surely return to you when life is due,*
*and behold, your wife Sarah will have a son!'"*

**1** *Devarim:* Hebrew for "things."

**2** We have learned that the expression *It came to pass...:* This derives from the Talmud.

**3** The lowest of all upper rungs...*Devarim: Shekhinah* is called *Davar,* "word" of God, since She conveys the divine essence. *Davar,* in Hebrew, means both "word" and "thing." Here the plural, *devarim,* from the verse in Genesis, is applied to *Shekhinah.*

**4** *I am not a man of* devarim, *words:* At the beginning of his career, Moses humbly acknowledges his speech impediment, but if we understand that *devarim* also refers to *Shekhinah,* we see that Moses also denies any intimacy with Her.

**5** Elohim...the evil impulse came to accuse...: The divine name *Elohim* is associated with *Din,* the divine attribute of Judgment. Here it also alludes to the evil impulse, a harsh manifestation of *Din* who appears outside the divine realm, *after...*devarim, the rung of *Shekhinah.* According to the Talmud, Satan accused Abraham of neglecting God, so God responded by commanding Abraham to sacrifice Isaac and thereby prove his devotion and zeal. Here Rabbi Shim'on suggests that the evil impulse is working for *Elohim:* his accusation is actually part of the divine plan, a mystical and psychological challenge to Abraham.

# 8 ☐ The Binding of Abraham and Isaac

*things*

*It came to pass after these* devarim[1] *that Elohim tested Abraham.*
*He said to him, "Abraham!"*
*and he answered, "Here I am."*
*He said, "Take your son, your only one, whom you love, Isaac,*
*and go forth to the land of Moriah*
*and offer him up there as an ascent-offering."*

—GENESIS 22:1–2

Rabbi Shim'on said,
"We have learned
that the expression *It came to pass in the days of* denotes sorrow,
while the phrase *It came to pass,* even without *in the days of,*
is tinged with sorrow.[2]

"*It came to pass after* the lowest of all upper rungs.
Who is that? *Devarim,*[3] *Shekhinah*
as is said: *I am not a man of* devarim, *words* (Exodus 4:10).[4]
Who came after this rung?
Elohim *tested Abraham,*
for the evil impulse came to accuse
in the presence of the blessed Holy One.[5]

31

6   Isaac was already thirty-seven years old: According to rabbinic tradition.

7   He had to be encompassed by judgment…: Through discovering God and expressing love, Abraham had attained the rung of *Hesed* (Love), but he was devoid of its complementary opposite: *Din* (Judgment). Being too one-sided, he now had to balance love with rigor in order to round out his personality and become a complete human being in the image of God.

8   Water was embraced by fire: Water and fire symbolize the pair of opposite *sefirot: Hesed* and *Din. Hesed* is free-flowing love; *Din* is the purgative power of judgment.

9   To execute judgment, arraying it in its realm: By binding Isaac on the altar, Abraham manifested the quality of *Din* both on earth and in the sefirotic realm.

10   One was judged, one executed judgment…: As Isaac submits to Abraham, they enact the drama of the *sefirot* together.

"Here we should contemplate: Elohim *tested Abraham.*
The verse should read: *tested Isaac,*
since Isaac was already thirty-seven years old[6]
and his father was no longer responsible for him.
If Isaac had said, 'I refuse,'
his father would not have been punished.
So why is it written: Elohim *tested Abraham,* and not Elohim *tested Isaac?*

"But *Abraham,* precisely!
For he had to be encompassed by judgment,
since previously Abraham contained no judgment at all.[7]
Now water was embraced by fire.[8]
Abraham was incomplete until now
when he was crowned to execute judgment, arraying it in its realm.[9]
His whole life long he was incomplete until now
when water was completed by fire, fire by water.

"So Elohim *tested Abraham, not Isaac,*
calling him to be embraced by judgment.
When he did so, fire entered water, becoming complete.
One was judged, one executed judgment, encompassing one another.[10]
Therefore the evil impulse came to accuse Abraham,
who was incomplete until he had executed judgment upon Isaac.
For the evil impulse appears *after* devarim, coming to accuse.

11 *Tested* et *Abraham—et*, precisely!: Grammatically, the word *et* is an accusative particle. It has no independent meaning and is lost in translation, but in rabbinic tradition it often amplifies the original meaning of a biblical verse. Here, *et* (spelled with the two Hebrew letters *alef* and *tav*) symbolizes *Shekhinah*, who comprises the entire alphabet of divine speech, from *alef* to *tav*.

12 This is Isaac, for at that time he dwelled in low power: Isaac was destined to rise to the *sefirah* of high power *(Gevurah* [Power], or *Din)*, but before he was bound on the altar he was unfulfilled, inhabiting the lower *sefirah* of *Shekhinah*, who derives from *Gevurah* and is indicated by *et*.

13 He was crowned in his realm alongside Abraham: Having undergone harsh judgment, Isaac manifests *Din* alongside Abraham, who manifests *Hesed*.

14 Then division became apparent: water versus fire: The two Patriarchs and their respective *sefirot* have completed one another, but they are not yet harmonized.

15 Until Jacob appeared...: Jacob, the third Patriarch (son of Isaac, grandson of Abraham) symbolizes the *sefirah* of *Tif'eret* (Beauty, Harmony). He was able to balance the polarity of *Hesed* and *Din*, Abraham and Isaac.

"Come and see the mystery of the word:
Although we have said that *Abraham* is written, not *Isaac*,
Isaac is encompassed by this verse through the mysterious wording:
Elohim *tested* et *Abraham*.
It is not written: *tested Abraham*,
but rather: *tested* et *Abraham*—*et*, precisely![11]
This is Isaac, for at that time he dwelled in low power.[12]
As soon as he was bound on the altar,
initiated into judgment fittingly by Abraham,
he was crowned in his realm alongside Abraham,[13]
fire and water encompassing one another, ascending.
Then division became apparent: water versus fire.[14]

"Who would have created a compassionate father who turned cruel?
It was only so division would manifest:
water versus fire, crowned in their realms,
until Jacob appeared and everything harmonized,
triad of Patriarchs completed, above and below arrayed."[15]

**1** These on the right, those on the left: Life is a balance between the flow of love *(Hesed)* from the right and the force of limitation *(Din)* from the left.

**2** From a single aspect through two well-known rungs: Prophecy is the result of divine emanation. The pair of lower *sefirot, Netsah* (Endurance) and *Hod* (Majesty), are the channels of inspiration, the field of prophetic vision.

**3** The mirror that does not shine: *Shekhinah* is known as the unclear mirror reflecting divine essence to the prophet. According to the Talmud, "All the prophets gazed through an opaque glass; Moses our Rabbi gazed through a translucent glass." In the New Testament Paul says, "For now we see through a glass darkly, but then face to face."

**4** A mirror in which all colors appear: The Hebrew word *mar'ah* means both "vision" and "mirror." *Shekhinah* is a mirror reflecting all the other *sefirot* to the gaze of the prophet, though not with full clarity.

# 9 □ Joseph's Dream

*Joseph dreamed a dream and told it to his brothers,*
*and they hated him even more.*

—GENESIS 37:5

Rabbi Hiyya opened,
*"He said, 'Hear my words:*
*If there be a prophet among you,*
*I, YHVH, make Myself known to him in a vision,*
*I speak with him in a dream'* (Numbers 12:6).

"Come and see how many rungs upon rungs
the blessed Holy One has fashioned,
arranged one atop the other, step by step,
this one higher than that one,
these absorbing those, as they should,
these on the right, those on the left,[1]
each assigned its domain, all fittingly.

"Come and see:
All prophets of the world were nurtured from a single aspect
through two well-known rungs.[2]
Those rungs appeared in the mirror that does not shine,[3]
as is written:                                    — *shekhinah*
*I make Myself known to him in* mar'ah, *a vision.*
What is this *mar'ah?*
It has been explained: a mirror in which all colors appear.[4]
This is the mirror that does not shine.

37

**5** One-sixtieth of prophecy…: According to the Talmud, "Fire is one-sixtieth of hell; honey is one-sixtieth of manna; the Sabbath is one-sixtieth of the world that is coming; sleep is one-sixtieth of death; a dream is one-sixtieth of prophecy."

**6** The sixth rung from the rung of prophecy: From the level of prophecy to the level of dream there are six stages, represented by the *sefirot* of *Netsah, Hod, Yesod,* and *Shekhinah,* and the angels Michael and Gabriel.

**7** Gabriel, appointed over dreams: In the Book of Daniel (8:16; 9:22), Gabriel is the angel who interprets dreams. Here he appears as prince of dreams.

**8** False imaginings intermingling…: Gabriel is located on a level beneath *Shekhinah,* outside the realm of the purely divine, where demonic forces lurk. These are the forces that smuggle false images into dreams. According to Rabbi Shim'on bar Yohai in the Talmud, "As there can be no grain without straw, so there can be no dream without absurdities."

**9** Follow the interpretation of the mouth: Of the interpreter.

**10** Speech commands that rung: *Shekhinah,* who expresses divine language, rules over Gabriel, prince of dreams. Human interpretation is effective because it activates the divine realm of Speech, who then translates the dream into reality.

*"I speak with him in a dream.*
This is one-sixtieth of prophecy, as they have established.[5]
It is the sixth rung from the rung of prophecy,[6]
rung of Gabriel, appointed over dreams.[7]
This has already been said.

"Come and see:
Every proper dream issues from this rung;
so you cannot have a dream without false imaginings intermingling,
as we have established.[8]
So parts are true and parts are false.
You cannot have a dream that does not reflect both this side and that.

"Since everything is contained in a dream, as we have said,
all dreams of the world follow the interpretation of the mouth.[9]
They have established this based on the verse:
*As he interpreted for us, so it came to pass* (Genesis 41:13).
Why?
Because a dream includes illusion and truth,
and the word rules over all.
So a dream needs a good interpretation."

Rabbi Yehudah said,
"Because every dream is from that lower rung,
and Speech commands that rung;[10]
that is why every dream follows the interpretation."

He opened and said,
*"In a dream, a vision of the night,*
*when slumber falls on humans*
*as they sleep upon their bed,*
*He uncovers human ears,*
*terrifies them with warning* (Job 33:15–16).

**11** Enthrone and accept the Kingdom of Heaven…a verse of mercy…: The first action refers to the bedtime recital of Shema, a central Jewish prayer declaring: "Hear O Israel, *YHVH* is our God, *YHVH* is One" (Deuteronomy 6:4). The second refers to Psalm 31:6: *Into Your hand I entrust my spirit; You redeem me,* YHVH, *faithful God.*

**12** She ascends…: The soul is depicted as feminine.

**13** Things corresponding to the mind's reflections: As taught by Rabbi Yonatan in the Talmud: "A person is shown only what is suggested by the reflections of his mind."

"Come and see:
When a person climbs into bed,
first he must enthrone and accept the Kingdom of Heaven,
then recite a verse of mercy,
as the Companions have established.[11]
For when a person sleeps in his bed,
his soul leaves him and soars up above,
each on its own path.
She ascends in this way, as has been said.[12]
What is written?
*In a dream, a vision of the night,*
when people are lying in their beds asleep,
the soul leaves them, as is written:
*as they sleep upon their bed, He uncovers human ears.*
Then the blessed Holy One reveals to the soul,
through that rung presiding over dreams,
things destined to come about in the world
or things corresponding to the mind's reflections,[13]
so the dreamer will respond to the warning.

"For nothing is revealed
while a person is still under the spell of the body,
as we have said.
Rather, an angel tells the soul,
and the soul, the person,
and that dream is from beyond,
when souls leave bodies and ascend,
each on its own path.

"There are rungs upon rungs within the mystery of a dream,
all within the mystery of wisdom.
Now come and see:
Dream, one rung,

**14** For twenty-two years it was delayed: The dream that Joseph told his brothers is related in Genesis 37:7: *We were binding sheaves in the field, when suddenly my sheaf stood upright; and behold, your sheaves gathered around and bowed down to mine!* According to the Talmud, it took twenty-two years for this dream to be fulfilled, that is, for Joseph's brothers to bow down to him (as related in Genesis 42:6).

**15** They provoked accusations against him: Their hatred stimulated demonic forces to delay the fulfillment of the dream.

vision, one rung,

prophecy, one rung.

All rungs upon rungs, one above the other.

*"Joseph dreamed a dream and told it to his brothers. . .*

*and they hated him even more because of his dreams* (Genesis 37:5, 8).

From here we learn

that a person should tell his dream only to one who loves him.

Otherwise the listener interferes,

and if that dream is transformed, he is the cause.

"Come and see:

Joseph told the dream to his brothers,

and they made the dream disappear;

for twenty-two years it was delayed."[14]

Rabbi Yose said, "How do we know this?

Because it is written: *They hated him even more.*

This implies that they provoked accusations against him.[15]

What is written?

*He said to them, 'Please hear this dream that I have dreamed'* (Genesis 37:6).

He begged them to listen;

then he revealed the dream to them.

If they had transformed its meaning,

it would have come true according to their words.

But they responded:

*'Will you reign over us?*

*Will you rule over us?'* (Genesis 37:8).

Suddenly they had revealed the interpretation of the dream

and sealed their own fate!

That is why *they hated him even more."*

✦ With the light created by God during the six days of Creation
Adam could see from one end of the world to the other.
God hid the light away for the righteous in the hereafter.
Where did He hide it?
In the Torah.
So when I open *The Book of Zohar* I see the whole world.

—Israel son of Eli'ezer, the *Ba'al Shem Tov* (eighteenth century)

# 10 □ Jacob's Garment of Days

*The days of Israel drew near to die.*
—GENESIS 47:29

Rabbi Yehudah opened,
*"Listen, you deaf ones!*
*You blind ones, look up and see!* (Isaiah 42:18).
*Listen, you deaf ones!*
you human beings who do not hear Torah speaking,
who do not open your ears to let in the commands of your Lord.
*You blind ones*
who do not examine your own foundations,
who do not seek to know why you are alive!
Every single day a herald comes forth and proclaims,
but no one hears his message!

"It has been taught:
When a human being is created,
on the day he comes into the world,
simultaneously, all the days of his life are arranged above.
One by one, they come flying down into the world
to alert that human being, day by day.
If, when a day comes to alert him,
he sins on that day before his Lord,
then that day climbs up in shame,
bears witness and stands alone outside.

1   The outlaw spirit: The demonic forces.

2   Missing from the total: Of fulfilled days.

3   When those days draw near to the Holy King: When one is about to die, as indicated in the verse that appears at the beginning of this *Zohar* passage: *The days of Israel drew near to die.*

4   They become a radiant garment for his soul!: The days that a person has filled with good deeds are woven into a garment of splendor, which will clothe the soul as she enters God's presence in the world to come. Similarly, according to Mahayana Buddhism, upon attaining Nirvana, Buddha receives "a special body created from his virtues."

"It has been taught:
After standing alone
it sits and waits for that human to turn back to his Lord,
to restore the day.
If he succeeds, that day returns to its place;
if not, that day comes down to join forces with the outlaw spirit,[1]
molding itself into an exact image of that human,
moving into his house to torment him.
Sometimes his stay is for the good,
if one purifies himself.
If not, it is a horrible visitation.
Either way, such days are lacking, missing from the total.[2]
Woe to the human being
who has decreased his days in the presence of the Holy King,
who has failed to reserve days up above—
days that could adorn him in that world,
days that could usher him into the presence of the Holy King!

"Come and see:
When those days draw near to the Holy King,[3]
if the person leaving the world is pure
he ascends and enters into those days
and they become a radiant garment for his soul![4]
But only his days of virtue, not his days of fault.
Woe to him who has decreased his days up above!
For when he comes to be clothed in his days,
the days that he ruined are missing
and he is clothed in a tattered garment.
It is worse if there are many such days;
then he will have nothing to wear in that world!
Woe to him! Woe to his soul!
He is punished in hell for those days,

**5** The mystery of our Mishnah: In fact, what follows is a kabbalistic homily with no basis in the Mishnah. The *Zohar* uses this linguistic formula to mask the contemporary teaching in the guise of ancient tradition.

**6** The radiant garment...had faded away: Adam and Eve's sin was so great that their entire fabric of days was ruined.

**7** *Garments of skin...:* Adam and Eve were originally clothed in garments of "light" (Hebrew, *or,* spelled with the letter *alef*), befitting their high spiritual nature. As a result of their sin, they fell into a lower, physical form and were clothed in garments of "skin" (*or,* spelled with the letter *ayin*).

**8** *He came into days:* The Hebrew, *ba ba-yamim* is an expression usually translated "advanced in days/years," although here it is understood literally.

days upon days,
two days for every wasted day!
For when he left this world, he found no days to wear,
he had no garment for cover.

"Happy are the righteous!
Their days are all stored up with the Holy King,
woven into radiant garments to be worn in the world that is coming.
We have learned in the mystery of our Mishnah:[5]
Why is it written:
*They knew that they were naked* (Genesis 3:7)?
Adam and Eve knew the naked truth:
the radiant garment woven from their days had faded away.[6]
Not one single day was left to wear,
as is written:
*Your eyes saw my unformed limbs,*
*in Your book they were all recorded.*
*The days that were fashioned—*
*not one of them is left* (Psalm 139:16).
Exactly!
Not one of those fashioned days was left to be worn.
And so it remained
until Adam made the effort to turn back to God and mend his ways.
The blessed Holy One accepted him
and made him different garments but not from his days,
as is written:
YHVH Elohim *made garments of skin for Adam and his wife*
*and He clothed them* (Genesis 3:21).[7]

"Come and see:
Abraham, who was pure, what is written of him?
*He came into days* (Genesis 24:1).[8]
When he left this world

9  Job.... No garment was left for him to wear: The biblical character Job is criticized in the *Zohar* for denying resurrection and questioning God's justice.

10  All who have a garment will be resurrected, as is written...: God's revelation to Job out of the whirlwind implies that without a garment, one cannot rise from the dead.

11  Crowned...with crowns worn by the Patriarchs...: According to Rav in the Talmud, "[In] the world that is coming...the righteous sit with crowns on their heads and bask in the splendor of *Shekhinah*." Here the "crowns worn by the Patriarchs" are the *sefirot* associated with Abraham, Isaac, and Jacob *(Hesed, Gevurah,* and *Tif'eret)*. The "stream that flows" is the flow of emanation that fills *Shekhinah,* who is the mystical Garden of Eden.

12  *Satisfy your soul with sparkling flashes:* The phrase is normally translated: *satisfy your thirst* [nefesh] *in parched places* [tsahtsahot]. *Nefesh* means both "soul" and "thirst"; the root of *tsahtsahot* means both "dazzling" and "parched." According to the *Zohar,* sparkling flashes enlighten the righteous soul in the world that is coming.

he entered into his very own days and put them on to wear.
Nothing was missing from that radiant garment:
*He came into days.*
But what is written of Job?
*He said, 'Naked I came from my mother's womb*
*And naked will I return there'* (Job 1:21).
No garment was left for him to wear.[9]

"It has been taught:
Happy are the righteous,
for their days are pure and extend to the world that is coming.
When they leave this world, all their days are sewn together,
made into radiant garments for them to wear.
Arrayed in that garment,
they are admitted into the world that is coming
to enjoy its pleasures.
Clothed in that garment,
they are destined to come back to life.
All who have a garment will be resurrected,
as is written:
*They will rise as in a garment* (Job 38:14).[10]
Woe to the wicked of the world,
whose days are faulty and full of holes!
There is not enough to cover them when they leave the world.

"It has been taught:
All the righteous
who are privileged to wear a radiant garment of their days
are crowned in that world with crowns worn by the Patriarchs
from the stream gushing forth into the Garden of Eden,[11]
as is written:
YHVH *will guide you always*
*and satisfy your soul with sparkling flashes* (Isaiah 58:11).[12]

**13** He attained…: Jacob's life was the culmination of the lives of the Patriarchs, and upon his death he was arrayed in the *sefirah* of *Tif'eret* (Beauty), which harmonizes the *sefirot* of Abraham and Isaac, *Hesed* and *Gevurah*.

But the wicked of the world,
unfit to wear a garment of days,
of them is written:
*He will be like a bush in the desert,*
*unaware of the coming of good,*
*inhabiting scorched wilderness* (Jeremiah 17:6)."

Rabbi Yitshak said,
"Happy is the destiny of Jacob!
He had such faith that he could say:
*'I will lie down with my fathers'* (Genesis 47:30).
He attained their level, nothing less!
He surpassed them, dressed in his days and in theirs!"[13]

**1** Anokhi, *I:* This is the first word spoken by God at the Revelation on Mount Sinai: *I am* YHVH *your God.* What follows is an interpretation of the revelation of divine speech, based on the account in Exodus.

**2** A spark flashed out to engrave: The divine spark, the first impulse of emanation, engraved the letters of the Ten Commandments on the stone tablets.

**3** A flowing measure...ten cubits...comets, seventy-one: The numbers correspond to the numerical value of the Hebrew word *Anokhi. Yod,* the final letter, equals ten; the other three letters *(alef, nun, kaf)* total seventy-one.

**4** On this side...on the other side...on every side: According to Rabbi Simai in the Talmud, all four sides of each stone tablet were engraved.

**5** From the side of the south...back to the south...: The Midrash explains that at Sinai the voice of God moved from the south to the north, to the east, to the west, in order to amaze the people of Israel. They ran from one direction to the next trying to locate the voice. Finally they exclaimed: *Wisdom, where can she be found?* (Job 28:12).

# 11 □ All of Israel Saw the Letters

Anokhi, *I*[1]
—EXODUS 20:2

Secret of secrets for those who know wisdom:
The moment these letters came forth,
secretly circling as one,
a spark flashed out to engrave.[2]
A flowing measure extended ten cubits on this side,
and out shot comets inside comets, seventy-one.[3]
Sparks burst into flashes, up high, down below,
quieting down, rising up high, beyond, beyond.
The flow measured out ten cubits on the other side,
and comets shot out in colors as before.
And so on every side.[4]

The spark expanded, whirling round and round.
Sparks burst into flashes and rose high above.
The heavens blazed with all their powers;
everything flashed, sparkled as one.
Then the spark turned from the side of the south
and outlined a curve from there to the east
and from east to north
until it circled back to the south as before.[5]
Then the spark swirled, disappearing;
comets and flashes dimmed.

**6** From the flowing measure of the spark: At Creation, and again at Sinai, God manifests Himself through the alchemy of letters.

Now they came forth, these carved, flaming letters
flashing like gold when it dazzles.
Like a craftsman smelting silver and gold:
when he takes them out of the blazing fire,
all is bright and pure;
so the letters came forth, pure and bright
from the flowing measure of the spark.[6]
So it is written:
*The word of* YHVH *is refined* (Psalm 18:31),
as silver and gold are refined.
When these letters came forth, they were all refined,
carved precisely, sparkling, flashing.
All of Israel saw the letters
Flying through space in every direction,
engraving themselves on the tablets of stone.

**1** The face of *Shekhinah:* The Talmud teaches that "whoever receives the face of his teacher [i.e., welcomes him], it is as if he receives the face of *Shekhinah....*One who receives the face of his friend, it is as if he receives the face of *Shekhinah.*" Here Rabbi Yose deletes the "as if," identifying his companion, Rabbi Hiyya, with the Divine Presence. As explained elsewhere in the *Zohar,* the Companions "are called the face of Shekhinah because Shekhinah is hidden within them. She is concealed and they are revealed."

**2** An old man, a donkey driver: The old man is an archetype of wisdom who appears frequently in the Zohar in the guise of a foolish donkey driver.

**3** 'Who is a serpent...': These riddles confuse not only Rabbi Yose; the cryptic language is intended to mystify the reader as well. Much of the imagery in the first two riddles alludes to various stages in the process of *gilgul* (reincarnation), one of the most esoteric doctrines of the *Zohar.* The riddle of the ravishing maiden is expounded later in the passage.

# 12 □ The Old Man and the Ravishing Maiden

Rabbi Hiyya and Rabbi Yose met one night at the Tower of Tyre.
They stayed there as guests, delighting in each other.
Rabbi Yose said, "I am so glad to see the face of *Shekhinah!*[1]
For just now, the whole way here, I was pestered by an old man,
a donkey driver,[2] who kept asking me riddles the whole way:

"'Who is a serpent that flies in the air and wanders alone,
while an ant lies peacefully between its teeth?
Beginning in union, it ends in separation.

"'Who is an eagle that nests in a tree that never was?
Its young who have been plundered,
who are not created creatures,
lie somewhere uncreated.
Going up, they come down; coming down, they go up.
Two who are one, and one who is three.

"'Who is a ravishing maiden without eyes,
her body concealed and revealed?
She comes out in the morning and is hidden all day.
She adorns herself with adornments that are not.'[3]

"All this he asked on the way; I was annoyed.
Now I can relax!
If we had been together, we would have engaged in words of Torah,
instead of strange words of chaos."

4   "Now two are three, and three are like one!": The old man and the two rabbis form a triad, recalling his earlier reference to "one who is three," yet also alluding to three parts of the soul, described elsewhere by the old man.

Rabbi Hiyya said, "That old man, the donkey driver,
do you know anything about him?"

Rabbi Yose replied, "I know that there is nothing in his words.
If he knew anything, he should have opened with Torah;
then the way would not have been empty!"

Rabbi Hiyya said, "That donkey driver, is he here?
For sometimes in those empty fools, you discover bells of gold!"

Rabbi Yose said, "Here he is, fixing some food for his donkey."

They called him, and he came over.
He said to them, "Now two are three, and three are like one!"**4**

Rabbi Yose said, "Didn't I tell you that all his words are empty nonsense?"

He sat before them and said,
"Rabbis, I turned into a donkey driver only a short time ago.
Before, I wasn't one.
But I have a small son, and I put him in school;
I want him to engage in Torah.
When I find one of the rabbis traveling on the road,
I guide his donkey from behind.
Today I thought that I would hear new words of Torah,
but I haven't heard anything!"

Rabbi Yose said, "Of all the words I heard you say,
there was one that really amazed me.
Either you said it out of folly, or they are empty words."

The old man said, "And which one is that?"

He said, "The one about the ravishing maiden."

**5** YHVH *is on my side...*: The old man, about to reveal secrets of Torah, begins by invoking divine protection and help. In the presence of rabbis who have not proven themselves, he has misgivings about the venture. The quotation also reflects the hesitancy of the author of the *Zohar* to publish the secrets. For him, the human threat is posed by opponents of Kabbalah or by other kabbalists who might disapprove of his undertaking.

**6** *I have placed My bow in the cloud:* This verse appears at the end of the story of Noah and the Flood, when God places a rainbow in the sky as a symbol of His promise never to destroy the earth again. The prophet Ezekiel (1:28) compares the Divine Presence to *the appearance of the rainbow in the clouds.* In the *Zohar*, Rainbow is one of the many names for *Shekhinah*, who displays all the colors of the *sefirot*.

**7** We have learned that the rainbow...: *Shekhinah* (the rainbow) takes off Her garment (the cloud) and gives it to Moses. Shielded by this cloud, he ascends Mount Sinai and encounters the beyond.

The old man opened and said,
"YHVH *is on my side; I have no fear.*
*What can any human do to me?*
YHVH *is by my side, helping me. . .*
*It is good to take refuge in* YHVH (Psalm 118:6–8).[5]

"How good, pleasant, precious, and high are words of Torah!
But how can I say them in front of rabbis
from whose mouths, until now, I haven't heard a single word?
But I should say them
because there is no shame at all in saying words of Torah
in front of everyone!"

The old man covered himself.
The old man opened and said,
"*Moses went inside the cloud and ascended the mountain* (Exodus 24:18).
What is this cloud?
The same one of which is written:
*I have placed My bow in the cloud* (Genesis 9:13).[6]
We have learned that the rainbow took off her garments
and gave them to Moses.[7]
Wearing that garment, he went up the mountain;
from inside it he saw what he saw,
delighting in the all, up to that place."

The Companions approached
and threw themselves down in front of the old man.
They cried and said, "If we have come into the world
only to hear these words from your mouth,
it is enough for us!"

The old man said,
"Companions, not for this alone did I begin the word.
An old man like me doesn't rattle with just a single word.

**8** No one near him sees or reflects: This is apparently the meaning of the phrase in the old man's riddle "a ravishing maiden without eyes"; that is, no eyes behold her.

Human beings are so confused in their minds!
They do not see the way of truth in Torah.
She calls out to them every day, in love,
but they do not want to turn their heads.
She removes a word from her sheath,
is seen for a moment, then quickly hides away,
but she does so only for those who know her intimately.

"A parable:
To what can this be compared?
To a beloved, ravishing maiden, hidden deep within her palace.
She has one lover, unknown to anyone, hidden too.
Out of love for her, this lover passes by her gate constantly,
lifting his eyes to every side.
Knowing that her lover hovers about her gate constantly,
what does she do?
She opens a little window in her hidden palace,
revealing her face to her lover,
then swiftly withdraws, concealing herself.
No one near him sees or reflects,[8] only the lover,
and his heart and his soul and everything within him
flow out to her.
He knows that out of love for him,
she revealed herself for that one moment
to awaken love in him.

"So it is with a word of Torah:
she reveals herself to no one but her lover.
Torah knows that one who is wise of heart
hovers about her gate every day.
What does she do?
She reveals her face to him from the palace
beckoning him with a hint,

**9** *Derasha:* The "search" for meaning. Also known as midrash, this is the second, deeper level of meaning in Torah, after the literal *(peshat)* sense. Through applying various hermeneutical techniques together with imagination, the interpreter expands the meaning of the biblical text.

**10** *Haggadah:* Literally, "telling," this refers to the third level of meaning, the allegorical level.

**11** All her hidden secrets: The mystical dimension of Torah, the highest level and deepest layer of meaning.

**12** Withholding nothing, concealing nothing: This explains the cryptic phrase in the old man's riddle "She adorns herself with adornments that are not." The initial encounter with Torah yields an apparent meaning that is found to be merely an adornment or disguise. Seeing through this garment, the mystic discovers the naked reality of revelation.

then swiftly withdraws to her hiding place.
No one there knows or reflects—
he alone does,
and his heart and his soul and everything within him
flows out to her.
This is why Torah reveals and conceals herself.
With love she approaches her lover
to arouse love with him.

"Come and see the way of Torah.
At first, when she begins to reveal herself to a human,
she beckons him with a hint.
If he perceives, good;
if not, she sends him a message, calling him simple.
Torah says to her messenger:
'Tell that simple one to come closer, so I can talk with him.'
He approaches.
She begins to speak with him from behind a curtain she has drawn,
words he can follow, until he reflects a little at a time.
This is *derasha*.⁹
Then she converses with him through a veil,
words riddled with allegory.
This is *haggadah*.¹⁰

"Once he has grown accustomed to her,
she reveals herself face to face
and tells him all her hidden secrets,¹¹
all the hidden ways,
since primordial days secreted in her heart.

"Now he is a complete human being,
husband of Torah, master of the house.
All her secrets she has revealed to him,
withholding nothing, concealing nothing.¹²

**13** Now the *peshat* of the verse…: The root *phst* means "to strip, make plain, explain." The *peshat* is the plain meaning, often contrasted with deeper layers of meaning. Here, though, the old man points to the paradox of mystical study. The *peshat* is the starting point, the word on the page. As meaning unfolds, layer by layer, one encounters the face of Torah. This is revelation, enlightenment. But in Kabbalah, enlightenment leads back to the word; the *peshat* reappears as the upshot. One emerges from the mystical experience of Torah with a profound appreciation of her textual form. As in the Zen koan: "First there is a mountain; then there is no mountain; then there is."

**14** Yeiva Sava: Yeiva the Elder. The old man finally reveals his name.

"She says to him, 'Do you see that word,
that hint with which I beckoned you at first?
So many secrets there! This one and that one!'

"Now he sees that nothing should be added to those words
and nothing taken away.
Now the *peshat* of the verse, just like it is.[13]
Not even a single word should be added or deleted.

"Human beings must become aware,
pursuing Torah to become her lovers!"

The old man was silent for a moment.
The Companions were amazed;
they did not know if it was day or night,
if they were really there or not.

"Enough, Companions!
From now on, you know that the evil side has no power over you.
I, Yeiva Sava,[14] have stood before you
to awaken your awareness of these words."

They rose as if awakened from sleep
and threw themselves down in front of him,
unable to utter a word.
After a while they began to cry.
Rabbi Hiyya opened and said,
*"Set me as a seal upon your heart,
as a seal upon your arm* (Song of Songs 8:6).
Love and sparks from the flame of our heart will escort you.
May it be the Will
that our image be engraved in your heart
as your image is engraved in ours."

He kissed them and blessed them, and they left.

✦ Whoever delves into the mysteries of the cosmos cannot help but stumble, as is written: *This stumbling block is in your hand* (Isaiah 3:6). One cannot grasp these things without stumbling over them.

—*Sefer ha-Bahir* ("The Book of Brightness") (twelfth century)

When they rejoined Rabbi Shim'on
and told him everything that happened,
he was delighted and amazed.
He said, "You are so fortunate to have attained all this!
Here you were with a heavenly lion,
a fierce warrior for whom many warriors are nothing,
and you could not recognize him!
I am amazed that you escaped being punished by him.
The blessed Holy One must have wanted to save you."

He called out these verses for them:
*"The path of the righteous is like gleaming light,*
*shining ever brighter until full day* (Proverbs 4:18).
*When you walk, your stride will be free;*
*if you run, you will not stumble* (Proverbs 4:12).
*Your people, all of them righteous, will inherit the land forever—*
*sprout of My planting, work of My hands, in which I glory* (Isaiah 60:21)."

**1** *Have them make Me a holy place, and I will dwell in their midst:* When the Israelites were wandering in the desert, God asked them to offer a gift, a contribution of precious materials for the construction of the *mishkan,* the "Dwelling" for God's presence.

**2** The plain by the Sea of Ginnosar: The Sea of Ginnosar is the Sea of Galilee, Lake Kinneret. The narrow plain on its northwestern shore is very fertile.

**3** We have already established the meaning of this verse: The verse from Song of Songs is cited in the Midrash as an account of the construction of the *mishkan* and the Temple in Jerusalem.

**4** The palace below, resembling the palace on high: *Shekhinah,* last of the *sefirot,* is the palace below. She resembles Her mother, *Binah,* the palace on high. So for the *Zohar,* the Dwelling constructed in the desert symbolizes a higher Dwelling, *Shekhinah,* who is sustained by the highest Dwelling, *Binah.*

**5** Garden of Eden...: *Shekhinah* is the mystical Garden of Eden, situated above and beyond the physical Garden of Eden. In His Garden, the blessed Holy One communes with the souls of the righteous. *Eden* in Hebrew means "pleasure, delight."

# 13 □ The Gift of Dwelling

*YHVH spoke to Moses, saying,*
*"Speak to the children of Israel and have them take Me a gift.*
*From everyone whose heart moves him take My gift....*
*Have them make Me a holy place, and I will dwell in their midst."*
—EXODUS 25:1–2, 8[1]

Rabbi Shim'on, Rabbi El'azar, Rabbi Abba, and Rabbi Yose
were sitting one day beneath some trees
on the plain by the Sea of Ginnosar.[2]
Rabbi Shim'on said,
"The shade spread over us by these trees is so pleasant!
We should crown this place with words of Torah!"

Rabbi Shim'on opened,
*"King Solomon made himself a pavilion from the trees of Lebanon*
(Song of Songs 3:9).
We have already established the meaning of this verse,[3]
but the pavilion is the palace below
resembling the palace on high.[4]
The blessed Holy One calls it Garden of Eden,
for He planted it for His pleasure and His yearning
to delight in the souls of the righteous,
all enrolled within.[5]
These are souls who have no body in this world.

73

6  Loveliness of *YHVH:* The phrase derives from Psalm 27:4: *One thing I ask of* YHVH, *that alone do I seek: to live in the house of* YHVH *all the days of my life, to gaze upon the loveliness of* YHVH *and to frequent His palace.* In the *Zohar,* "Loveliness of *YHVH*" refers to *Binah.*

7  Rivers of pure balsam: According to rabbinic tradition, thirteen rivers of balsam await the righteous in the world that is coming.

8  The trees of the pavilion…: The *sefirot* from *Hesed* to *Yesod,* out of which the pavilion *(Shekhinah)* is made. Rabbi Shim'on yearns for the shade of these higher *sefirot.*

9  The synagogue: The modern place of Jewish worship takes the place of the desert Dwelling.

10  On the level of *Tsaddiq…:* Hebrew for "righteous," referring to *Yesod,* the ninth *sefirah,* who unites with *Shekhinah.*

11  When the blessed Holy One comes to synagogue…ten people…: A quorum of ten, called a *minyan,* is required for public prayer. This talmudic passage suggests that without a *minyan,* God would be in no mood for union.

They all ascend, where they are crowned.
They have sites from which to gaze,
enjoying the joy on high, called Loveliness of *YHVH*.[6]
There they are filled by precious flows of rivers of pure balsam.[7]

"Whoever attains the pavilion is entitled to everything.
He is worthy of sitting in the comfort of the shade of the blessed Holy One,
as is said: *I delight to sit in his shade* (Song of Songs 2:3).
Now that we are sitting in this shade of comfort,
we should be aware that we are sitting in the shade of the blessed Holy One
within the pavilion!
We should crown this place with crowns so high
that the trees of the pavilion will be swayed
to cover us with further shade.[8]

"Happy is the Holy People!
Their Lord searches for them, calls to them
to bring them close to Him.
So the Holy People should join together and enter the synagogue.[9]
Whoever arrives earliest joins himself to *Shekhinah* in a single bond!

"Come and see:
The first one present in the synagogue, happy is his portion!
He stands on the level of *Tsaddiq*, together with *Shekhinah*.[10]
This is the secret meaning of:
*Those who seek Me early will find Me* (Proverbs 8:17).
This one ascends very high!

"Now you might say, 'But we have learned:
"When the blessed Holy One comes to synagogue
and does not find ten people there,
He instantly turns angry!"[11]
How can you say that one who comes early
joins himself to *Shekhinah* and stands on the level of *Tsaddiq*?'

✦ Something you cannot explain to another person is called *nistar*, "hidden," like the taste of food, which is impossible to describe to one who has never tasted it. You cannot express in words exactly what it is—it is hidden. Similarly with the love and awe of God: it is impossible to explain to another what the love in your heart feels like. This is hidden.

But calling the wisdom of Kabbalah "hidden" is strange. How is it hidden? Whoever wants to learn—the book is readily available. If one does not understand, he is ignorant. For such a person, the Talmud is also hidden! Rather, the secrets hidden throughout the *Zohar* are based entirely on cleaving to God.

—Menahem Mendel of Peremishlany (eighteenth century)

"A parable:
There was a king
who ordered all the inhabitants of the city to appear in his presence
on a certain day, at a certain place.
While the people were preparing themselves,
one came early to that place.
Meanwhile, the king appeared and found the person who had arrived early.
He said, 'You! Where are all my subjects?'
He answered, 'My Lord, I have come early,
but they are coming behind me, according to the command of the king.'
The king was pleased,
sat down with him and conversed with him;
he became the king's beloved.
Meanwhile, all the people arrived.
The king was appeased and sent them in peace.
But if they had not arrived,
if one had not come early to represent them,
to tell the king that all of them were on the way,
the king would have instantly turned angry.

"Here too, since one comes early and is present in the synagogue
and *Shekhinah* comes and finds him,
it is considered as if all of them were present
because this one is waiting for them.
At once *Shekhinah* joins Herself to him;
they sit in a single coupling.
She comes to know him intimately and seats him on the level of *Tsaddiq*.
But if no one comes early,
if no one is present,
what is written?
*Why have I come? There is no man!* (Isaiah 50:2).
The verse does not read: *There are not ten.*

12  *Man of* Elohim: Moses is described as such in Deuteronomy 33:1,
which the *Zohar* takes to mean "husband of *Shekhinah.*" Here Rabbi
Shim'on indicates that any man who comes early to synagogue imitates
Moses by joining with *Shekhinah.*

13  In the shade of the Tree of Life in the Garden of Eden: The Tree of
Life symbolizes *Tif'eret,* also called the Written Torah. Torah is identified with the Tree of Life, based on the description of wisdom in
Proverbs 3:18: *She is a tree of life to those who grasp her.* As noted
above, the Garden of Eden symbolizes *Shekhinah.*

14  The paths that guard this tree: Paths of *Shekhinah,* the Oral Torah,
which protect, preserve, and expand the Written Torah.

15  It was difficult for him; he was unable to understand…: According to
the Talmud, "Three things were too difficult for Moses to understand
until the blessed Holy One showed him with His finger: the *menorah,*
[recognizing] the new moon, and [determining which] creeping creatures [were pure and which were impure]."

16  If this gift was given by the blessed Holy One to Moses alone: The
gift is *Shekhinah.*

It reads: *There is no man!*
to join himself to Me, to be with Me,
as is said: *man of* Elohim (Deuteronomy 33:1),[12]
to be on the level of *Tsaddiq.*"

Rabbi Shim'on rose, and the Companions too.
They rose and walked on.
Rabbi El'azar said to Rabbi Shim'on, his father,
"Father, until now we have been sitting
in the shade of the Tree of Life in the Garden of Eden![13]
From now on, since we are walking,
we should follow the paths that guard this tree."[14]

Rabbi Abba opened,
"*Have them take Me a gift. From everyone. . .*
When the blessed Holy One showed Moses the work of the Dwelling,
it was difficult for him; he was unable to understand.[15]
This has been established.
Now *we* have to raise a difficulty:
If this gift was given by the blessed Holy One to Moses alone,[16]
how could He give Her to another?
How could He say that the children of Israel should take this gift?
Ah, but of course He gave Her to Moses, not to anyone else!

"A parable:
There was a king among his people,
but the queen was not with the king.
As long as the queen was not with the king,
the people did not feel secure;
they could not dwell safely.
As soon as the queen came,
all the people rejoiced and dwelled safely.

**17** *Have them take My gift: I place My Dwelling in your midst!:* Following his parable, Rabbi Abba reinterprets God's command in Exodus 25:2 not as *Have them take Me a gift,* but rather *Have them take My gift,* implying that *Shekhinah,* the gift, is given *by* God, not *to* God. She is the Queen, wedded to Moses, but dwelling among all the people. To support his interpretation, Rabbi Abba adds a verse from Leviticus (26:11): *I place My Dwelling in your midst.* The *Dwelling (mishkan)* is *Shekhinah* Herself.

**18** *Moses consummated... the Bride of Moses...:* Hebrew, *kallot Mosheh, kallat Mosheh.* Rabbi Abba links the word *kallot* (to consummate, complete) with the word *kallah* (bride), suggesting that the bride is *Shekhinah,* who is married to Moses, husband of *Elohim.* Half-human, half-divine, Moses consummates the ritual union of God. The reader is left wondering who the king in the parable represents, God or Moses?

**19** A generation like this will not arise...: According to the *Zohar,* the generation of Rabbi Shim'on is the holiest one that will ever be, until the Messiah appears. Consequently, Rabbi Shim'on and his Companions can discover and reveal even the deepest mystical secrets.

**20** Torah has been restored to her ancientry!: Rabbi Shim'on's exclamation cryptically conveys the goal and method of the *Zohar:* to reinstate the authority of tradition by creating "new-ancient" mythical teachings and transmitting them through talmudic figures.

"So at first, even though the blessed Holy One
performed miracles and signs through Moses,
the people did not feel secure.
As soon as the blessed Holy One said
*Have them take My gift: I place My Dwelling in your midst!*[17]
everyone felt secure and rejoiced in the ritual of the blessed Holy One,
as is written:
*On the day that Moses consummated setting up the Dwelling* (Numbers 7:1),
for the Bride of Moses came down to earth!"[18]

Rabbi Shim'on cried and said,
"Now I know for sure
that supernal Holy Spirit reverberates within you.
Happy is this generation!
A generation like this will not arise until King Messiah appears![19]
Torah has been restored to her ancientry![20]
Happy are the righteous
in this world and in the world that is coming!"

**1** She is Sabbath: *Shekhinah* is the Sabbath Queen, entering the palace of time every Friday evening at sunset. As the seventh *sefirah* below *Binah* (the Divine Mother), *Shekhinah* is also the seventh primordial day. Friday night is the time of Her union with Her male counterpart, *Tif'eret,* so the Sabbath is God's wedding celebration.

**2** United in the secret of one...: *Shekhinah* and the angels accompanying Her join together, just as *Tif'eret* joins the *sefirot* surrounding Him, before the divine couple unites. Each must achieve wholeness before uniting with the other.

**3** The Other Side: The demonic realm, which threatens *Shekhinah* and humanity during the other six days of the week. Once Sabbath begins, *Shekhinah* is safe and showers the world with blessing.

**4** She is crowned over and over to face the holy King: The Sabbath is described as Queen already in the Talmud: "Rabbi Hanina used to wrap himself in a garment, stand close to sunset as Sabbath entered, and exclaim, 'Come, let us go out to welcome Sabbath the Queen!' Rabbi Yannai would put on special clothes as Sabbath entered and exclaim, 'Come, O bride! Come, O bride!'" Here in the *Zohar,* Queen *Shekhinah* prepares to meet King *Tif'eret.* Later, this wedding imagery inspired a sixteenth-century kabbalist, Solomon Alkabez, to compose *Lekhah Dodi,* a poem that has become the highlight of the Friday evening service and whose refrain is: "Come, my beloved, to greet the bride! Let us welcome the presence of Sabbath!"

82

# 14 □ The Secret of Sabbath

The Secret of Sabbath:
She is Sabbath![1]
United in the secret of one,
drawing upon Her the secret of one.[2]

When Sabbath enters She is alone,
separated from the Other Side,[3]
all judgments removed from Her.
Basking in the oneness of holy light,
She is crowned over and over to face the holy King.[4]

5 All powers of wrath…: Once Sabbath has entered, the power of strict judgment disappears. According to the Talmud, even the wicked in hell are granted rest on the Sabbath.

6 Crowned with new souls: Rabbi Shim'on son of Lakish taught that "the blessed Holy One gives a person an extra soul on Sabbath eve. When Sabbath departs, it is taken away." This extra soul enables one to leave weekday concerns behind and experience the joy and depth of the Sabbath. In the words of the *Zohar*, "Every Friday evening, a person sits in the world of souls."

All powers of wrath and masters of judgment flee from Her.[5]
There is no power in all worlds aside from Her.
Her face shines with a light from beyond;
She is crowned below by the holy people,
all of whom are crowned with new souls.[6]
Then the beginning of prayer,
blessing Her with joy, with beaming faces.

**1** *Ein Sof:* Literally, this phrase means "there is no end." *Ein Sof* is the Absolute, God as infinite, beyond any of the specific qualities of the *sefirot.*

**2** Primordial Nothingness: The highest *sefirah, Keter,* borders on Infinity and cannot be comprehended by rational thought. Source of all being, it transcends normal being and is paradoxically called Nothingness—a creative pool of Nothingness.

**3** Highest point, beginning of all: The second *sefirah, Hokhmah,* is the first that can be conceived in any way and is pictured as a point of light emerging from the nothingness of *Keter.* See chapter 3, n. 7.

**4** Culmination of the word: This phrase, from Ecclesiastes 12:13, here designates *Shekhinah,* last of the *sefirot,* the culmination of divine emanation and speech.

**5** No end: Hebrew, *Ein Sof.*

**6** Infinity: Hebrew, *Ein Sof.*

**7** All these lights and sparks…: The nine lower *sefirot* are generated and sustained by the emanation of *Ein Sof,* but even they cannot comprehend Infinity.

## 15 ☐ The Aroma of Infinity

*Ein Sof*[1] does not abide being known,
does not produce end or beginning.
Primordial Nothingness[2] engendered beginning and end.
Who is beginning?
Highest point, beginning of all,[3]
concealed one abiding in thought.
It also yields end, culmination of the word.[4]
But there, no end.[5]
No desires, no lights, no sparks in that Infinity.[6]
All these lights and sparks are dependent on It
but cannot comprehend.[7]

**8** Highest desire…: The highest *sefirah (Keter),* also called *Ratson* (Will, Desire), is supremely hidden and indescribably aware of *Ein Sof.*

**9** The world that is coming: The rabbinic concept of *ha-olam ha-ba* is often understood as referring to the afterlife and is usually translated as "the world to come." However, it can also be seen and rendered from another perspective as "the world that is coming," already existing, though in another dimension. The *Zohar* identifies "the world that is coming" with *Binah,* the Divine Mother who flows and engenders the seven lower *sefirot.* She is "the world that is coming, constantly coming and never ceasing." Here *Binah* ascends with *Hokhmah* toward *Ein Sof.*

The only one who knows, yet without knowing,
is highest desire, concealed of all concealed, Nothingness.[8]
And when the highest point and the world that is coming[9] ascend,
they know only the aroma,
as one inhaling an aroma is sweetened.

1 | Mishkan: "Dwelling, abode," the Tabernacle constructed by Israel in the desert. See chapter 13.

# 16 ☐ God, Israel, and Shekhinah

*If you follow My decrees*
*and observe My commands and carry them out...*
*I will place My* mishkan[1] *in your midst*
*and My soul will not abhor you.*
*I will move about in your midst:*
*I will be your God, and you will be My people....*

*But if you spurn My decrees,*
*and if your soul abhors My judgments,*
*so that you do not carry out My commands,*
*so that you break My covenant...*
*I will set My face against you:*
*you will be routed by your enemies*
*and your foes will dominate you.*
*You will flee though none pursues.*
*And if, for all that, you do not obey Me...*
*I will discipline you Myself, seven for your sins...*
*and I will scatter you among the nations....*

*Yet even at this point,*
*when they are in the land of their enemies,*
*I will not spurn them or abhor them so as to destroy them,*
*breaking My covenant with them,*
*for I am YHVH, their God.*

LEVITICUS 26, PASSIM

**2** My *mishkan* is *Shekhinah*, My *mishkan* is My *mashkon*...: Both *mishkan* and *Shekhinah* share the root *shkhn*, meaning "to dwell." *Shekhinah* is God's indwelling Presence that accompanied Israel through the desert in the *mishkan* and later dwelled in the Temple in Jerusalem. The Midrash links the word *mishkan* with *mashkon*, "pledge." Both the desert Tabernacle and the Temple are a pledge offered by the people as a guarantee of their loyalty to God and His commandments. "If they [Israel] sin, the holy Temple will be seized on their account, as is said: *I will place My* mishkan *in your midst*. Do not read: *My* mishkan, but rather: *My* mashkon."

**3** My *mashkon*, literally Mine!: After citing the midrashic play on words, the *Zohar* presents its own version: the *mashkon*, the pledge, is offered by God, not Israel, as explained in the following parable.

**4** He took His most precious possession: The blessed Holy One (*Tif'eret*) took *Shekhinah*.

**5** Has removed Himself...let Him come and dwell among us!: Although God has placed Israel in exile, He left *Shekhinah* with them. In the words of Rabbi Shim'on bar Yohai, "Come and see how beloved are Israel in the sight of the blessed Holy One! Wherever they went in exile, *Shekhinah* accompanied them." Possessing God's feminine half, the Jewish people hold collateral, a guarantee that He will always return to them and to His beloved.

*I will place My* mishkan *in your midst.*
My *mishkan* is *Shekhinah,*
My *mishkan* is My *mashkon,*
My dwelling is My pledge,
who has been seized on account of Israel's sins.[2]

*I will place My* mishkan.
My *mashkon*, literally Mine![3]
A parable:
One person loved another, and said,
"My love for you is so high I want to live with you!"
The other said, "How can I be sure you will stay with me?"
So he took all his most precious belongings
and brought them to the other, saying,
"Here is a pledge to you that I will never part from you."

So the blessed Holy One desired to dwell with Israel.
What did He do?
He took His most precious possession[4]
and brought it down to them, saying,
"Israel, now you have My pledge; so I will never part from you."

Even though the blessed Holy One has removed Himself from us,
He has left a pledge in our hands,
and we guard that treasure of His.
If He wants His pledge, let Him come and dwell among us![5]

So *I will place My* mishkan *in your midst*
means: "I will deposit a *mashkon* in your hands
to ensure that I will dwell with you."
Even though Israel is now in exile,
the pledge of the blessed Holy One is with them,
and they have never forsaken it.

**6** He took his bed…: The bed is a symbol of intimacy and stability.

**7** Here, My Bed is in your house!: *Shekhinah* is symbolized by a bed, indicating Her intimate relationship with *Tif'eret,* the blessed Holy One. The medieval monk Peter Damian writes that Mary was the golden couch upon which God, tired out by the actions of humanity, lay down to rest.

**8** The Sea of Tiberias: The Sea of Galilee.

**9** They rose at midnight: According to the Talmud, King David used to rise at midnight. "There was a harp suspended above David's bed. As soon as midnight arrived, a north wind came and blew upon it, and it played by itself. He immediately arose and engaged in Torah until the break of dawn." In the *Zohar,* this legendary custom is expanded into a ritual: all kabbalists are expected to rise at midnight and adorn *Shekhinah* with words of Torah and song in preparation for Her union with *Tif'eret.* This parallels the midnight vigil, common among medieval Christian monks. In fact, elsewhere in the *Zohar,* Rabbi Yehudah alludes to the Christian practice: "I have seen something similar among the nations of the world."

**10** The Tree of Life: Torah is identified with the Tree of Life, based on the description of wisdom in Proverbs 3:18: *She is a tree of life to those who grasp her.* Tree of Life is also a name for *Tif'eret,* who is symbolized by the Written Torah.

*And My soul will not abhor you.*
A parable:
One person loved his friend and wanted to live together.
What did he do?
He took his bed and brought it to his friend's house.[6]
He said, "My bed is now in your house,
so I will not go far from you or your bed or your things."

So the blessed Holy One said,
*"I will place My Dwelling in your midst*
*and My soul will not abhor you.*
Here, My Bed is in your house![7]
Since My Bed is with you, you know I will not leave you:
*My soul will not abhor you."*

*I will move about in your midst: I will be your God.*
Since *My Dwelling* is with you,
you can be certain that I will go with you,
as is written:
*For YHVH your God moves about in your camp*
*to deliver you and deliver your enemies to you:*
*let your camp be holy* (Deuteronomy 23:15).

One night, Rabbi Yitshak and Rabbi Yehudah
were staying in a village near the Sea of Tiberias.[8]
They rose at midnight.[9]
Rabbi Yitshak said to Rabbi Yehudah, "Let us converse in words of Torah,
for even though we are in this place,
we must not separate ourselves from the Tree of Life."[10]

**11**  *The Tent…*: The Tent of Meeting, the *mishkan,* symbolizing *Shekhinah.*

**12**  Exchanged His Glory…in the hands of a trustee…: By worshiping the Golden Calf at Mount Sinai, Israel exchanged God's Glory *(Shekhinah)* for a mere idol, thereby forfeiting their claim to the pledge. Moses, seeking to keep that pledge from returning immediately to God, transferred it to a third party, Joshua.

**13**  Because he was to Moses as the moon is to the sun: According to the Talmud, "The face of Moses was like the face of the sun; the face of Joshua was like the face of the moon." The moon symbolizes *Shekhinah,* and Joshua shares that symbol with Her.

Rabbi Yehudah opened,

"*Moses took the Tent and pitched it outside the camp* (Exodus 33:7).[11]

Why?

Moses said to himself,

'Since Israel has dealt falsely with the blessed Holy One

and exchanged His Glory,

let His pledge be placed in the hands of a trustee

until we see with whom it remains.'[12]

He said to Joshua,

'You will be the trustee between the blessed Holy One and Israel.

The pledge will remain in your trust

and we will see with whom it remains.'

What is written?

*And he* [Moses] *returned to the camp,*

*but his attendant, Joshua the son of Nun, a youth,*

*did not stir out of the Tent* (Exodus 33:11).

Why Joshua?

Because he was to Moses as the moon is to the sun.[13]

He was worthy to guard the pledge;

so he *did not stir out of the Tent.*

"The blessed Holy One said to Moses,

'Moses, this is not right!

I have given My pledge to them!

Even though they have sinned against Me,

the pledge must remain with them so that I will not leave them.

Do you want Me to depart from Israel and never return?

Return My pledge to them,

and for its sake I will not abandon them, wherever they are.'

"Even though Israel has sinned against God,

they have not abandoned this pledge of His,

and the blessed Holy One has not taken it from them.

**14** So with Israel…: The parable and the analogy do not correspond exactly. In the parable, the pledge is the son, who guarantees the king's faithfulness and love for the queen. In the analogy, the pledge is *Shekhinah,* the Queen, who guarantees God's love for Israel, the son. The *Zohar* is tingling the reader's mind, subtly introducing puzzling questions: Who is a pledge for whom? What is the relationship between Israel and *Shekhinah,* the mystical Assembly of Israel?

So wherever Israel goes in exile, *Shekhinah* is with them.
Therefore it is written: *I will place My* mishkan *in your midst.*
This has been established."

Rabbi Yitshak opened,
"*My beloved is like a gazelle, like a young deer.*
*There he stands behind our wall,*
*gazing through the windows, peering through the holes* (Song of Songs 2:9).

"Happy are Israel!
They are privileged to hold this pledge of the Supreme King!
For even though they are in exile,
every new moon and Sabbath and festival
the blessed Holy One comes to watch over them,
gazing at His pledge that is with them, His treasure.
A parable:
There was a king whose queen offended him.
He expelled her from the palace.
What did she do?
She took his son, his precious beloved.
Since the king was fond of her, he let him go with her.
When the king began to yearn for the queen and her son,
he climbed up on roofs, ran down stairs, scaled walls;
he peered through the holes in the walls just to see them!
When he caught a glimpse of them
he started to cry from behind the wall.
Then he went away.

"So with Israel:
Even though they have left the palace of the King,
they have not abandoned that pledge.
And since the King loves them, He has left it with them.[14]
When the Holy King begins to yearn for the Queen and for Israel,

**15** As is written: *My beloved is like a gazelle...*: Rabbi Yitshak imitates the Midrash on Song of Songs, which interprets this and many other verses as love poetry between Israel and God.

**16** A synagogue must have windows: According to Rabbi Yohanan in the Talmud, "A person should only pray in a house with windows."

He climbs up on roofs, runs down stairs, scales walls;
He peers through the holes in the walls just to see them!
When He catches a glimpse of them, He starts to cry.
As is written:
*My beloved is like a gazelle, a young deer,*
jumping from wall to roof, from roof to wall.
*There he stands behind our wall*
in the synagogues and houses of study.[15]
*Gazing through the windows,*
for indeed, a synagogue must have windows.[16]
*Peering through the holes*
to look at them, to look after them.

"So Israel should rejoice on that day,
for they know this, and they say:
*This is the day* YHVH *has made—*
*let us rejoice and be happy!* (Psalm 118:24)."

*But if you spurn My decrees. . .*
Rabbi Yose opened,
*"My son, do not spurn the discipline of* YHVH,
*do not dread His correction* (Proverbs 3:11).
How beloved are Israel to the blessed Holy One!
He wants to correct them and guide them in a straight path
like a father who loves his son:
because of his love for him, there is a rod in his hand
to guide him in a straight path
so that he will not stray to the right or the left;
as is written: YHVH *corrects the one He loves,*
*as a father, the son he delights in* (Proverbs 3:12).

**17** *I have loved you*...: This verse is spoken to the people Israel, represented by Jacob.

**18** *But Esau I hated, so I removed the rod from him*...: See Proverbs 13:24: *He who withholds the rod hates his son.* Esau, Jacob's twin brother, symbolizes medieval Christendom. This passage is a veiled commentary on the condition of the Jews in Christian Spain: whereas Christianity claimed that Israel's poor situation was a sign of divine punishment for their rejection of Christ, the *Zohar* sees its people's suffering as a sign of God's loving discipline. Esau's rise to power, on the other hand, is evidence that God has forsaken him and offers him no correction.

**19** *Through other deputies*...: Powers of harsh judgment.

**20** *Myself. Now I will confront you! Seven*...: *Shekhinah* is called "I" or "Myself," the immediate presence of God. She is also the last of the seven lower *sefirot* and includes them all, so She is called Seven. Here the point is that She will discipline the people of Israel directly.

"One who is not loved by the blessed Holy One,
one hated by him—
correction is removed from him, the rod removed.
It is written: *I have loved you, says* YHVH (Malachi 1:2).[17]
Because of His love, there is always a rod in His hand to guide him.
*But Esau I hated* (Malachi 1:3),
so I removed the rod from him, removed correction,[18]
so as not to share Myself with him.
He is far from My soul,
but as for you, *I have loved you!*
*So, My son, do not spurn the discipline of* YHVH,
*do not dread His correction.*"

Rabbi Abba said,
"*I will discipline you Myself, seven for your sins.*
I disciplined you through other deputies,[19]
as has been established.
*Myself.*
Now I will confront you!
*Seven* will be aroused against you!"[20]

"Come and see the pure love of the blessed Holy One for Israel.
A parable:
There was a king who had a single son who kept misbehaving.
One day he offended the king.
The king said, 'I have punished you so many times
and you have not accepted the reprimand.
Now look, what should I do with you?
If I banish you from the land and expel you from the kingdom,
perhaps wild beasts or wolves or robbers will attack you
and you will be no more.
What can I do?
The only solution is that I and you together leave the land!'

21   *Myself* too, along with you!: Rabbi Abba understands the verse to mean: *I will discipline you and Myself!*

22   *For your crimes, your Mother was sent away:* In this verse from Isaiah, the "mother" is Israel personified; here in the *Zohar,* She is *Shekhinah.* According to another passage in the *Zohar, Shekhinah* is banished because She failed to discipline Her son, Israel.

"So, *Myself:* 'I and you together will leave the land!'
The blessed Holy One said as follows:
'Israel, what should I do with you?
I have already punished you, and you have not heeded Me.
I have brought fearsome warriors and flaming forces to strike at you
and you have not obeyed.
If I expel you from the land alone,
I fear that packs of wolves and bears will attack you
and you will be no more.
But what can I do with you?
The only solution is that I and you together leave the land
and both of us go into exile.
As is written: *I will discipline you,*
forcing *you into exile;*
but *if you think that I will abandon you—*
*Myself too, along with you!*[21]

"*Seven for your sins.*
This means Seven, who will be banished along with you.
Why? *For your sins,*
as is written: *For your crimes, your Mother was sent away* (Isaiah 50:1).[22]
The blessed Holy One said,
'You have made Me homeless as well as yourselves,
for the Queen has left the palace along with you.
Everything is ruined, My palace and yours!
For a palace is worthless to a king unless he can enter with his queen.
A king is only happy when he enters the queen's palace
and finds her with her son;
they all rejoice as one.
Now neither son nor queen is present;
the palace is totally desolate.
What can I do?
*I Myself will be with you!'*

**23** YHVH *your God will return*. *He Himself will return!...*: As recorded in the Talmud in the name of Rabbi Shim'on bar Yohai: "When they are destined to be redeemed, *Shekhinah* will be with them, as is said: YHVH *your God will return your captivity*. The verse does not read: *ve-heshiv* ['He will bring back'], but rather: *ve-shav* ['He will return']. This teaches that the blessed Holy One will return with them from amidst the exile."

**24** *The verse should read: I will not strike them or kill them...*: The verbs "strike" and "kill" seem to fit the context better.

**25** *My soul's beloved*: *Shekhinah*.

**26** *Le-khallotam: So as to destroy them*. But Rabbi El'azar reads the word as it is spelled.

**27** *Spelled: le-khalltam, without the o*: The letter *vav*, denoting the *o*, is not found here in the biblical text. This abbreviated spelling stimulates Rabbi El'azar to create a midrash.

**28** *The tanners' market*: Notorious for its foul odor. In the words of the Talmud, "Woe to him who is a tanner by trade!" According to the Mishnah, a woman can demand a divorce from her husband if he is a tanner.

"So now, even though Israel is in exile,

the blessed Holy One is with them and has not abandoned them.

And when Israel comes out of exile

the blessed Holy One will return with them,

as is written: YHVH *your God will return* (Deuteronomy 30:3).

He Himself will return!

This has already been said."[23]

Rabbi Hiyya and Rabbi Yose were walking on the road.

They happened upon a certain cave in a field.

Rabbi Hiyya said,

"I have heard a new word from Rabbi El'azar:

*'I will not spurn them or abhor them so as to destroy them.*

The verse should read:

*I will not strike them or kill them so as to destroy them.*[24]

But instead we find: *I will not spurn them or abhor them.*

Usually, one who is hated by another

is repulsive and utterly abhorrent to him,

but here: *I will not spurn them or abhor them.*

Why?

Because My soul's beloved[25] is among them

and because of Her, all of them are beloved to Me,

as is written: *le-khallotam,*[26]

spelled: *le-khalltam,* without the *o.*[27]

Because of Her, *I will not spurn them or abhor them,*

because She is the love of My life.

'A parable:

A man loved a woman.

She lived in the tanners' market.[28]

If she were not there, he would never enter the place.

Since she is there, it appears to him as a market of spice-peddlers

with all the world's finest aromas in the air.

29  Le-khallatam, *Because of their bride:* The abbreviated spelling enables
Rabbi El'azar to insert an *a* for the *o* and to read the word as le-khallatam,
*because of their bride,* instead of le-khallotam, *so as to destroy them.* For
a similar play on words, see the conclusion of chapter 13. The reader is
left wondering: Whose bride is *Shekhinah:* Israel's or God's? What does
it mean that *Shekhinah* is in our midst? What is the relationship between
God, Israel, and *Shekhinah*? See n. 14.

'Here too:
*Yet even at this point, when they are in the land of their enemies,*
which is a tanners' market,
*I will not spurn them or abhor them.*
Why?
Le-khallatam, *Because of their bride,*[29]
for I love Her!
She is the beloved of My soul dwelling there!
It seems filled with all the finest aromas of the world
because of the bride in their midst.'"

Rabbi Yose said,
"If I have come here only to hear this word, it is enough for me!"

1  Pinhas son of Ya'ir: A second-century figure renowned for his saint-
liness and ability to work miracles. According to the Talmud, he is Rabbi
Shim'on's son-in-law, but the *Zohar* promotes him to the rank of
father-in-law.

2  Ahiyah of Shiloh: The prophet who revealed that Solomon's kingdom
would be divided (see 1 Kings 11:29–39). According to rabbinic tradition, Ahiyah was a master of the secrets of Torah and the teacher of the
prophet Elijah. Later, he is portrayed as mentor of the *Ba'al Shem Tov*,
the founder of Hasidism.

3  Saw what he saw: A common phrase in the *Zohar* that alludes here
to seeing *Shekhinah* before one's death.

# 17 □ The Wedding Celebration

On the day Rabbi Shim'on was to leave the world,
while he was arranging his affairs,
the Companions assembled at his house.
Present were Rabbi El'azar, his son, Rabbi Abba, and the other Companions.
The house was full.
Rabbi Shim'on raised his eyes and saw that the house was filled.
He cried and said,
"The other time I was ill, Rabbi Pinhas son of Ya'ir[1] was in my presence.
I was already selecting my place in paradise next to Ahiyah of Shiloh[2]
when they extended my life until now.
When I returned, fire was whirling in front of me;
it has never gone out.
No human has entered without permission.
Now I see it has gone out, and the house is filled."

While they were sitting,
Rabbi Shim'on opened his eyes and saw what he saw;[3]
fire whirled through the house.
Everyone left;
Rabbi El'azar, his son, and Rabbi Abba remained;
the other Companions sat outside.
Rabbi Shim'on rose and laughed in delight.
He asked, "Where are the Companions?"
Rabbi El'azar rose and brought them in.
They sat in front of him.
Rabbi Shim'on raised his hands and prayed a prayer.

4 The threshing house: During an assembly at the threshing house, six of the Companions proved their mystical ability and stamina by surviving the overwhelming power of the revelations, while three others died. Now the six experienced Companions are invited back to hear Rabbi Shim'on's final words.

5 To enter without shame into the world that is coming: Displaying the knowledge of secrets prevents any feeling of shame.

6 A password…: Later Rabbi Shim'on explains, "All these words have been hidden in my heart until now. I wanted to hide them for the world that is coming, for there they ask a question and require wisdom of me. But now it is the will of the blessed Holy One [that I reveal these words]. Behold, without shame I will enter His palace!"

7 King Jeroboam: The first ruler of the northern kingdom of Israel, Jeroboam had golden calves built in Bethel and Dan to dissuade people from traveling to the Temple in Jerusalem in the southern kingdom of Judah. See 1 Kings 12:25–33.

Rejoicing, he said,

"Those Companions who were present at the threshing house[4] will convene
    here."

Everyone left;

Rabbi El'azar, his son, Rabbi Abba, Rabbi Yehudah,

Rabbi Yose, and Rabbi Hiyya remained.

Rabbi Abba sat behind him and Rabbi El'azar in front.

Rabbi Shim'on said, "Now is a time of favor.

I want to enter without shame into the world that is coming.[5]

Holy words, until now unrevealed,

I want to reveal in the presence of *Shekhinah*,

so it will not be said that I left the world deficiently.

Until now they were hidden in my heart

as a password to the world that is coming.[6]

I will arrange you like this:

Rabbi Abba will write; Rabbi El'azar, my son, will repeat;

the other Companions will meditate within."

Rabbi Abba rose from behind him;

Rabbi El'azar, his son, sat in front.

Rabbi Shim'on said, "Rise, my son,

for someone else will sit in that place."

Rabbi El'azar rose.

Rabbi Shim'on enwrapped himself and sat down.

He opened and said,

"It is so different now than at the threshing house.

There the blessed Holy One and His chariots convened.

Now He is accompanied by the righteous from the Garden of Eden!

This did not happen before.

The blessed Holy One wants the righteous to be honored

more than He wants Himself to be honored.

So it is written concerning King Jeroboam.[7]

8　Ido the prophet…: According to 1 Kings 13, a prophet from Judah came to Bethel and prophesied the destruction of King Jeroboam's altar. When the king heard this prophecy, *he stretched out his hand…and cried, "Seize him!" But his hand…dried up; he could not draw it back* (13:4). The name of the prophet is not mentioned, but he is traditionally identified as Ido.

9　Rav Hamnuna Sava: Rabbi Hamnuna the Elder, a Babylonian teacher of the third century, figures prominently in the *Zohar*.

10　The Holy Ancient One: The primal manifestation of *Ein Sof* (the Infinite) through the first *sefirah*, *Keter*.

11　The blessed Holy One: *Tif'eret*, the central *sefirah*, less concealed than the Holy Ancient One.

He offered incense to idols and worshiped them;
yet the blessed Holy One was patient.
But as soon as he stretched out his hand against Ido the prophet,
his hand dried up.[8]
Not because he worshiped idols,
but because he threatened Ido the prophet.
Now the blessed Holy One wants *us* to be honored
and all of them are coming with him!
Here is Rav Hamnuna Sava[9]
surrounded by seventy of the righteous adorned with crowns,
each one dazzling with the luster of the Holy Ancient One,[10]
concealed of all concealed.
He is coming to hear in joy these words I am about to speak!"

Rabbi Shim'on was about to sit down, when he exclaimed:
"Look! Here is Rabbi Pinhas son of Ya'ir!
Prepare his place!"
The Companions trembled;
they rose and moved to the periphery of the house.
Rabbi El'azar and Rabbi Abba remained with Rabbi Shim'on.

Rabbi Shim'on said,
"In the threshing house we were found to be:
all the Companions speaking, I among them.
Now I alone will speak;
all are listening to my words, those above and those below.
Happy is my share this day!"

Rabbi Shim'on opened and said,
"*I am my beloved's,
his desire is upon me* (Song of Songs 7:11).
All the days that I have been bound to this world
I have been bound in a single bond with the blessed Holy One.[11]

12 Nine lights: The nine *sefirot* that emanate from the Holy Ancient One.

13 Wedding celebration: Rabbi Shim'on's death is in fact a wedding because his soul is about to ascend and unite with *Shekhinah.*

14 Permission: To reveal it.

That is why now *his desire is upon me.*

He and His holy entourage have come to hear in joy concealed words
and praise for the Holy Ancient One, concealed of all concealed.

Separate, separated from all, yet not separate.

For all is joined to It, and It is joined to all.

It is all!

Ancient of all ancients, concealed of all concealed.

Arrayed and not arrayed.

Arrayed to sustain all;

not arrayed, for It is not to be found.

Arrayed, It radiates nine lights,[12]

blazing from It, from Its array.

Those lights, sparkling, flashing, emanate in every direction.

"Until now these words were concealed,
for I was scared to reveal;
now they have been revealed!
Yet it is revealed before the Holy Ancient One
that I have not acted for my own honor
nor for the honor of my family
but rather so I will not enter His palace in shame.
Furthermore, I see that the blessed Holy One
and all these righteous ones approve:
I see all of them rejoicing in this, my wedding celebration![13]
All of them are invited, in that world, to my wedding celebration.
Happy is my share!"

Rabbi Abba said,
"When the Holy Spark, the High Spark, finished this word
he raised his hands, cried and laughed.
He wanted to reveal one word.
He said, 'I have been troubled by this word all my days
and now they are not giving me permission!'[14]

**15** Will not miss its mark like the other day: At the earlier assembly in the threshing house, when the Companions participated in revealing secrets, the day was somehow incomplete.

**16** The High Spark: Above, this phrase denotes Rabbi Shim'on, while here it describes the Holy Ancient One, from whom emanate the nine lower *sefirot,* or "sparks."

**17** Adornments…Crowns…: The *Zohar* carefully avoids the common kabbalistic term *sefirot.*

"Summoning up his courage,
he sat and moved his lips and bowed three times.
No one could look at his place, certainly not at him.
He said, 'Mouth, mouth, you have attained so much!
Your spring has not dried up.
Your spring flows ceaselessly.
Of you is written:
*A river issues from Eden* (Genesis 2:10),
*Like a spring whose waters do not fail* (Isaiah 58:11).
Now I avow:
All the days I have been alive, I have yearned to see this day.
Now my desire is crowned with success.
This day itself is crowned.
Now I want to reveal words in the presence of the blessed Holy One;
all those words adorn my head like a crown.
This day will not miss its mark like the other day,[15]
for this whole day is mine.
I have now begun revealing words
so I will not enter shamefully into the world that is coming.
I have begun! I will speak!

'I have seen that all those sparks flash from the High Spark,[16]
hidden of all hidden.
All are levels of enlightenment.
In the light of each and every level
there is revealed what is revealed.
All those lights are connected:
this light to that light, that light to this light,
one shining into the other,
inseparable, one from the other.

The light of each and every spark,
called Adornments of the King, Crowns of the King—[17]

18 It and Its name is one: The *sefirot* are God's name, the expression of divine being.

19 Garment of the King: Another metaphor for the *sefirot.*

20 The Ineffable One, the Unrevealed: *Ein Sof,* the Infinite.

21 There is nothing but the High Spark…: Although the *sefirot* are rungs on the ladder to enlightenment, they lose their independent existence once one discovers through contemplation the ultimate reality of the High Spark.

each one shines into, joins onto the light within, within,
not separating without.
So all rises to one level,
all is crowned with one word;
no separating one from the other.
It and Its name is one.[18]

The light that is revealed is called Garment of the King.[19]
The light within, within is a concealed light.
In that light dwells the Ineffable One, the Unrevealed.[20]
All those sparks and those lights sparkle from the Holy Ancient One,
concealed of all concealed, the High Spark.
Upon reflecting,
all those lights emanating—
there is nothing but the High Spark, hidden, unrevealed.'"[21]

Rabbi Abba said,
"Before the Holy Spark finished, his words subsided.
I was still writing, intending to write more,
but I heard nothing.
I did not raise my head:
the light was overwhelming, I could not look.
Then I started trembling.
I heard a voice calling:
*Lengths of days and years of life* (Proverbs 3:2).
I heard another voice:
*He asked You for life, and You granted it* (Psalm 21:5).

"All day long, the fire in the house did not go out.
No one reached him; no one could:
light and fire surrounded him.
All day long, I lay on the ground and wailed.
After the fire disappeared

22 A litter of a ladder…: Intentionally cryptic. The "confusion" describes not only the Companions' state of mind following the death of Rabbi Shim'on, but also the deliberately confusing vocabulary.

23 Truculent stingers…from Sepphoris: Mighty Torah scholars from Sepphoris in the Galilee who wanted Rabbi Shim'on buried in their city, famed for its learning.

24 Meron: The site of Rabbi Shim'on's burial cave in Galilee.

I saw the Holy Spark, Holy of Holies, leaving the world,
enwrapped, lying on his right side, his face smiling.

"Rabbi El'azar, his son, rose, took his hands and kissed them.
As for me, I licked the dust from the bottom of his feet.
The Companions wanted to cry but could not utter a sound.
Finally they let out a cry,
but Rabbi El'azar, his son, fell three times, unable to open his mouth.
Finally he opened and cried, 'Father! Father!'"

Rabbi Hiyya rose to his feet and said,
"Until now the Holy Spark has looked after us;
now is the time to engage in honoring him."
Rabbi El'azar and Rabbi Abba rose.
They carried him on a litter of a ladder—
Who has seen Companions' confusion?—**22**
and fragrance wafted throughout the house.
They lifted him onto his bed;
only Rabbi El'azar and Rabbi Abba attended him.
Truculent stingers and shield-bearing warriors from Sepphoris**23**
came and beset them.
The people of Meron**24** banded together and shouted,
for they feared he would not be buried there.

After the bed emerged from the house, it rose into the air;
fire blazed before it.
They heard a voice:
"Come and enter!
Assemble for the wedding celebration of Rabbi Shim'on!
*He shall enter in peace;*
*they shall rest upon their couches* (Isaiah 57:2)."

✦ What should be your intention as you approach this wisdom?

Learning this wisdom for its own sake: to enter its mysteries, to know your Creator, to attain a wondrous level of comprehension of the Torah, to pray in the presence of your Creator, to unite the blessed Holy One and *Shekhinah* [the masculine and feminine aspects of God] by enacting the *mitsvot* [divine commandments]. This is the worship pleasing to God. Then you will walk the path safely. Faithfully God will make you aware of aspects of the divine Torah that no one else has yet attained. For each soul has a unique portion in the Torah.

Those who persevere in this wisdom find that when they ponder these teachings many times, knowledge grows within them—an increase of essence. The search always leads to something new.

—Moses Cordovero (sixteenth century)

As he entered the cave, they heard a voice from inside:
'This is the man who shook the earth, who made kingdoms tremble!
His Lord prides Himself on him every day.
Happy is his share above and below!
Countless sublime treasures lie in store for him.
*Go to the end and take your rest;*
*you will rise for your reward at the end of days (Daniel 12:13)."*

# ☐ Notes

## Chapter 1
1. " 'Master of wheat' means…": Babylonian Talmud, *Bava Batra* 145b.

## Chapter 2
4. Mishnah, *Avot* 3:14.
8. "The souls of all…": *Shemot Rabbah* 28:4.
10. "A cosmic body containing all souls": Babylonian Talmud, *Yevamot* 62a.

## Chapter 3
8. " 'The world was created through ten commands' ": Mishnah, *Avot* 5:1.

## Chapter 4
1. *Tanhuma, Shemini* 9, in the name of Rabbi Yehudah son of Shim'on.
2. " 'A thread-thin ray of love' ": Babylonian Talmud, *Hagigah* 12b.
"The Ba'al Shem Tov…": Benjamin Mintz, ed., *Shivehei ha-Besht* (Tel Aviv: Talpiyot, 1961), 79.

## Chapter 5
2. "It often amplifies…": Babylonian Talmud, *Pesahim* 22b; *Hagigah* 12a.
3. *Bereshit Rabbah* 21:8; *Seder Eliyahu Rabbah* 1; *Midrash ha-Gadol,* Genesis 3:24.
4. " 'I am *alpha* and *omega*' ": Revelation 1:8.
5. For further information, see Matt, *Zohar: The Book of Enlightenment,* 215–16.

## Chapter 6
2. Babylonian Talmud, *Yevamot* 62b.
3. " 'Rabbi El'azar said…' ": Babylonian Talmud, *Yevamot* 63a.
"Adam was created…": *Bereshit Rabbah* 8:1. See Matt, *Zohar: The Book of Enlightenment,* 217.

## Chapter 7

2. Babylonian Talmud, *Hagigah* 13b.
6. " 'You are alive…' ": Solomon ibn Gabirol, *Keter Malkhut,* 4.

## Chapter 8

2. Babylonian Talmud, *Megillah* 10b.
5. "Satan accused Abraham of neglecting God…": Babylonian Talmud, *Sanhedrin* 89b.
6. *Seder Olam Rabbah* 1; *Tanhuma, Vayera* 23; *Pirqei de-Rabbi Eli'ezer* 31.
11. "It often amplifies…": Babylonian Talmud, *Pesahim* 22b; *Hagigah* 12a.

## Chapter 9

3. " 'All the prophets gazed…' ": Babylonian Talmud, *Yevamot* 49b.
" 'For now we see…' ": 1 Corinthians 13:12.
5. Babylonian Talmud, *Berakhot* 57b.
8. " 'As there can be no grain without straw…' ": Babylonian Talmud, *Berakhot* 55a.
9. Babylonian Talmud, *Berakhot* 55b.
11. Babylonian Talmud, *Berakhot* 4b–5a.
13. Babylonian Talmud, *Berakhot* 55b.
14. "It took twenty-two years…": Babylonian Talmud, *Berakhot* 55b.

## Chapter 10

4. "Upon attaining Nirvana…": Gershom Scholem, *On the Mystical Shape of the Godhead,* 264–65.
5. See *Bereshit Rabbah* 19:6; *Pirqei de-Rabbi Eli'ezer* 14.
7. *Bereshit Rabbah* 20:12; *Zohar* 1:36b; 2:229b; 3:261b; Origen, *Contra Celsum* 4:40.
11. " '[In] the world…' ": Babylonian Talmud, *Berakhot* 17a.

## Chapter 11

4. Jerusalem Talmud, *Sheqalim* 6:1, 49d; Louis Ginzberg, *Legends of the Jews* (Philadelphia: Jewish Publication Society, 1968), 6:49, n. 258. See Exodus 32:15.
5. *Shemot Rabbah* 5:9.

## Chapter 12

1. "Whoever receives the face…": Jerusalem Talmud, *Eruvin* 5:1, 22b.
"The Companions 'are called…' ": *Zohar* 2:163b.

4. "Three parts of the soul": *Zohar* 2:100a.

12. "Seeing through this garment…": See chapter 2.

## Chapter 13

3. *Pesiqta de-Rav Kahana* 1:2; *Shir ha-Shirim Rabbah* and *Targum* on Song of Songs 3:9; *Zohar* 1:29a.

7. *Bereshit Rabbah* 62:2; Babylonian Talmud, *Ta'anit* 25a.

11. Babylonian Talmud, *Berakhot* 6b.

12. *Midrash Tehillim* 90:5; *Pesiqta de-Rav Kahana, nispahim, Vezot haberakhah,* 443–44, 448 (variants); *Tanhuma, Vezot haberakhah* 2; *Devarim Rabbah* 11:4; *Zohar* 1:21b, 148a, 236b; 239a; 2:22b.

13. See Babylonian Talmud, *Berakhot* 32b; 61b.

15. Babylonian Talmud, *Menahot* 29a.

17. Rabbi Abba's reinterpretation of Exodus 25:2 is based on *Vayiqra Rabbah* 30:12.

18. Rabbi Abba's pun derives from *Pesiqta de-Rav Kahana* 1:1, where Israel is described as the bride of God.

20. Rabbi Shim'on is paraphrasing Babylonian Talmud, *Qiddushin* 66a: "He restored Torah to her original state."

## Chapter 14

4. " 'Rabbi Hanina…' " Babylonian Talmud, *Shabbat* 119a.

5. "Even the wicked in hell…": Babylonian Talmud, *Sanhedrin* 65b.

6. "Rabbi Shim'on…": Babylonian Talmud, *Beitsah* 16a.
" 'Every Friday…' ": *Zohar* 2:136b.

## Chapter 15

9. " 'The world that is coming,' already existing": See *Tanhuma, Vayiqra* 8; Maimonides, *Mishneh Torah, Hilekhot Teshuvah* 8:8.
" 'The world that is coming, constantly coming and never ceasing' ": *Zohar* 3:290b.

## Chapter 16

2. " 'If they [Israel] sin…' ": *Shemot Rabbah* 31:9.

5. "'Come and see...'": Babylonian Talmud, *Megillah* 29a; *Mekhilta, Pisha* 14.

7. "Mary was the golden couch...": See Raphael Patai, *The Hebrew Goddess* (New York: KTAV, 1978), 258–59.

9. "'There was a harp...'": Babylonian Talmud, *Berakhot* 3b.
"'I have seen something similar...'": *Zohar* 3:119a.

10. Babylonian Talmud, *Berakhot* 32b; 61b.

12. "Israel exchanged God's Glory *(Shekhinah)* for a mere idol...": See Psalm 106:20: *They exchanged their Glory for the image of a bull.*

13. "'The face of Moses...'": Babylonian Talmud, *Bava Batra* 75a.

15. *Shir ha-Shirim Rabbah,* on Song of Songs 2:9.

16. Babylonian Talmud, *Berakhot* 34b.

22. "*Shekhinah* is banished...": *Zohar* 3:74a–b.

23. "'When they are destined to be redeemed...'": Babylonian Talmud, *Megillah* 29a; see *Mekhilta, Pisha* 14.

28. "'Woe to him who is a tanner by trade!'": Babylonian Talmud, *Qiddushin* 82b.
"A woman can demand...": Mishnah, *Ketubbot* 9:10.

## Chapter 17

1. Babylonian Talmud, *Shabbat* 33b.

2. On Ahiyah of Shiloh, see Babylonian Talmud, *Sanhedrin* 102a; Jerusalem Talmud, *Eruvin* 5:1, 22b; *Bereshit Rabbah* 35:2; *Midrash Tehillim* 5:8; Jacob Joseph of Polonoyye, *Toledot Ya'aqov Yosef* (Koretz, 1780), 156a.

4. The assembly at the threshing house is recounted in *Zohar* 3:127b–145a and known as *Idra Rabba* ("The Great [Assembly at the] Threshing House"). This section of the *Zohar,* "The Wedding Celebration" (3:287b–296b), is known as *Idra Zuta* ("The Small [Assembly at the] Threshing House").

6. *Zohar* 3:291a.

8. "He is traditionally identified as Ido": See Matt, *Zohar: The Book of Enlightenment,* 295.

22. On this bizarre phrase, see Matt, *Zohar: The Book of Enlightenment,* 298.

# ☐ Glossary

**Alef:** The first letter of the Hebrew alphabet.

**Ba'al Shem Tov:** Master of the Good Name; the title of Israel son of Eli'ezer, charismatic founder of Hasidism (ca. 1700–1760).

**Binah:** Understanding; the third *sefirah;* the Divine Mother who gives birth to the seven lower *sefirot.*

**Blessed Holy One:** Common rabbinic name for God. In the *Zohar* it often designates *Tif'eret.*

**Din:** Judgment; the fifth *sefirah;* the left arm of the divine body balancing *Hesed;* also called *Gevurah.* The roots of evil lie here.

**Ein Sof:** There is no end, the boundless, the Infinite; the ultimate reality of God beyond all specific qualities of the *sefirot.*

**Elohim:** God, gods, a biblical name for God. In the *Zohar* it is associated with various *sefirot: Binah, Gevurah, Shekhinah.*

**Gedullah:** Greatness; the fourth *sefirah;* the outpouring of God's great goodness; also called *Hesed.*

**Gevurah:** Power; the fifth *sefirah;* also called *Din.*

**Hasidism:** Popular religious movement that emerged in the second half of the eighteenth century in Eastern Europe; a popularization of Kabbalah.

**Hesed:** Love; the fourth *sefirah;* the right arm of the divine body balancing *Din;* also called *Gedullah.*

**Hod:** Majesty; the eighth *sefirah;* the left leg of the divine body; source of prophecy along with *Netsah.*

*Hokhmah:* Wisdom; the second *sefirah;* the original point of emanation.

**Holy Ancient One:** The primal manifestation of *Ein Sof* through *Keter,* Its Crown.

**Kabbalah:** Receiving, that which is handed down by tradition; Jewish mystical teaching.

*Keter:* Crown; the first *sefirah;* coeternal with *Ein Sof;* also called *Ratson* (Will) and *Ayin* (Nothingness).

*Malkhut:* Kingdom; the tenth *sefirah,* conveying the flow of emanation to the lower worlds; also called *Shekhinah.*

*Menorah:* Candelabrum of seven branches; prominent feature of the *mishkan.*

**Midrash:** Legal or homiletical interpretation of the biblical text.

*Mishkan:* God's dwelling in the desert; the Tabernacle constructed by the Israelites.

**Mishnah:** Collection of oral teachings edited near the beginning of the third century by Rabbi Yehudah Ha-Nasi.

*Mitsvah* **(pl.** *mitsvot***):** Divine commandment; one of the 613 commandments of the Torah; by extension: good deed.

*Netsah:* Endurance; the seventh *sefirah;* the right leg of the divine body; source of prophecy along with *Hod.*

**Oral Torah:** The interpretation of the Written Torah; in Kabbalah, a symbol of *Shekhinah.*

*Rahamim:* Compassion; the sixth *sefirah,* balancing *Ḥesed and Din;* also called *Tif'eret.*

*Sefirah* **(pl.** *sefirot***):** One of ten aspects of God's personality. See "Introduction to the *Zohar,"* p. xxii and pp. xxvi–xxix.

**Shekhinah:** Divine Presence; the tenth *sefirah;* female partner of *Tif'eret;* also called *Malkhut.*

**Talmud:** The Mishnah accompanied by a vast body of commentary and discussion by scholars of the third to sixth centuries.

*Tav:* The last letter of the Hebrew alphabet.

*Tif'eret:* Beauty; the sixth *sefirah;* male partner of *Shekhinah;* the trunk of the divine body; also called *Rahamim.*

**Torah:** Teaching; the first five books of the Bible; by extension: all religious teaching.

*Tsaddiq:* Righteous One; the ninth *sefirah, Yesod.*

**Written Torah:** The first five books of the Bible; in Kabbalah, a symbol of *Tif'eret.*

**Yesod:** Foundation; the ninth *sefirah,* who channels the flow of emanation to *Shekhinah;* also called *Tsaddiq.*

**YHVH:** The ineffable name of God; in the *Zohar* it is often associated with *Tif'eret.*

*Zohar:* Radiance, splendor.

*Zohar Hadash:* New *Zohar;* a collection of Zoharic texts found in manuscripts after the printing of the bulk of the *Zohar.* The title is misleading, since the volume contains much of *Midrash ha-Ne'lam,* the oldest stratum of the *Zohar.*

# Suggested Readings □

## Translations of the *Zohar*

Matt, Daniel C. *Zohar: The Book of Enlightenment*. The Classics of Western Spirituality. Mahwah, N.J.: Paulist Press, 1983. Annotated translations of selections from the *Zohar*.

———, trans. *The Zohar: Pritzker Edition*. 3 vols. (currently). Stanford: Stanford University Press, 2004–2005.

Sperling, Harry, and Maurice Simon, trans. *The Zohar*. 5 vols. London: Soncino Press, 1931–1934. A paraphrased translation of most of the *Zohar*.

Tishby, Isaiah, and Fischel Lachower. *The Wisdom of the Zohar: An Anthology of Texts*. 3 vols. Translated by David Goldstein. Oxford: Oxford University Press, 1989. Annotated translations arranged thematically, with masterful, extensive introductions.

## Other Works

Ariel, David. *The Mystic Quest: An Introduction to Jewish Mysticism*. New York: Schocken Books, 1992. A readable, comprehensive guide.

Fine, Lawrence, ed. *Essential Papers on Kabbalah*. New York: New York University Press, 1995. A stimulating collection of studies by leading scholars in the field.

———. "Kabbalistic Texts." In *Back to the Sources: Reading the Classic Jewish Texts*, edited by Barry W. Holtz, 304–39. New York: Summit Books, 1984. A clear, concise presentation of the development of Kabbalah and its symbolism.

Green, Arthur. *Ehyeh: A Kabbalah for Tomorrow*. Woodstock, Vt.: Jewish Lights, 2004. Explains how the ancient language of Kabbalah can be retooled to address the needs of our generation.

———. *A Guide to the Zohar*. Stanford: Stanford University Press, 2004.

———, ed. *Jewish Spirituality*. Vol. 1, *From the Bible through the Middle Ages*. Vol. 2, *From the Sixteenth-Century Revival to the Present*. New York: Crossroad Press, 1986, 1988. A stimulating collection of studies by prominent scholars.

Idel, Moshe. *Kabbalah: New Perspectives*. New Haven: Yale University Press, 1988. A groundbreaking, challenging work by a leading authority in the field.

Kaplan, Aryeh. *Meditation and Kabbalah*. York Beach, Me.: Samuel Weiser, 1982. A rich collection of texts presented by a practicing kabbalist.

Kushner, Lawrence. *Honey from the Rock: An Introduction to Jewish Mysticism*. Woodstock, Vt.: Jewish Lights, 2000. Quite simply, the easiest introduction to Jewish mysticism you can read.

―――. *The Way Into Jewish Mystical Tradition.* Woodstock, Vt.: Jewish Lights, 2001. Explains the principles of Jewish mystical thinking.

Liebes, Yehuda. *Studies in the Zohar.* Albany: State University of New York Press, 1993. Fascinating studies by a leading authority in the field.

Matt, Daniel C. *"Ayin:* The Concept of Nothingness in Jewish Mysticism." In Fine, *Essential Papers on Kabbalah,* 67–108.

―――. *The Essential Kabbalah: The Heart of Jewish Mysticism.* San Francisco: HarperSanFrancisco, 1995. Annotated translations of a wide range of kabbalistic texts arranged thematically.

―――. *God and the Big Bang: Discovering Harmony between Science and Spirituality.* Woodstock, Vt.: Jewish Lights, 1996. Uncovers how science and religion together can enrich our spiritual understanding.

―――. "The Mystic and the *Mitsvot."* In Green, *Jewish Spirituality: From the Bible through the Middle Ages,* 367–404. A study of the spiritual significance of religious action in Kabbalah.

―――. "New-Ancient Words: The Aura of Secrecy in the *Zohar."* In *Gershom Scholem's "Major Trends in Jewish Mysticism": Fifty Years After,* edited by Peter Schaefer and Joseph Dan, 181-207. Tübingen: J.C.B. Mohr (Paul Siebeck), 1994.

Scholem, Gershom. *Kabbalah.* Jerusalem: Keter, 1974. A collection of Scholem's articles from the *Encyclopaedia Judaica.* The most comprehensive single volume on Kabbalah, covering its historical development and major concepts and personalities.

―――. *Major Trends in Jewish Mysticism.* New York: Schocken, 1961. The classic work by the scholar who made Kabbalah accessible to the modern world.

―――. *On the Kabbalah and Its Symbolism.* New York: Schocken, 1965. Fascinating essays on Torah, myth, ritual, and other topics.

―――. *On the Mystical Shape of the Godhead.* New York: Schocken, 1991. Superb essays on *Shekhinah,* good and evil, transmigration, and other topics.

Wolfson, Elliot R. *Along the Path: Studies in Kabbalistic Myth, Symbolism and Hermeneutics.* Albany: State University of New York Press, 1995.

―――. *Circle in the Square: Studies in the Use of Gender in Kabbalistic Symbolism.* Albany: State University of New York Press, 1995. Two vibrant collections by a leading authority in the field.

―――. *Through a Speculum That Shines: Vision and Imagination in Medieval Jewish Mysticism.* Princeton: Princeton University Press, 1994. An enlightening treatment of visionary experience in a wide range of Jewish mystical texts.

# Index of *Zohar* Passages ☐

For readers who want to refer to the original Aramaic text of the *Zohar:*

* References are to the standard Aramaic edition of *Sefer ha-Zohar* in three volumes. 1: Genesis; 2: Exodus; 3: Leviticus, Numbers, Deuteronomy. *Zohar Hadash* is cited according to Re'uven Margaliot's edition (Jerusalem: Mosad ha-Rav Kook, 1978).

## *Spirituality*

**Next to Godliness:** Finding the Sacred in Housekeeping
*Edited and with Introductions by Alice Peck*
Offers new perspectives on how we can reach out for the Divine.
6 x 9, 224 pp, Quality PB, 978-1-59473-214-0 **$19.99**

**Bread, Body, Spirit:** Finding the Sacred in Food
*Edited and with Introductions by Alice Peck*
Explores how food feeds our faith.
6 x 9, 224 pp, Quality PB, 978-1-59473-242-3 **$19.99**

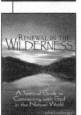

**Renewal in the Wilderness:** A Spiritual Guide to Connecting with God in the Natural World *by John Lionberger*
Reveals the power of experiencing God's presence in many variations of the natural world.
6 x 9, 176 pp, b/w photos, Quality PB, 978-1-59473-219-5 **$16.99**

**Honoring Motherhood:** Prayers, Ceremonies and Blessings
*Edited and with Introductions by Lynn L. Caruso*
Journey through the seasons of motherhood.
5 x 7¼, 272 pp, HC, 978-1-59473-239-3 **$19.99**

**Soul Fire:** Accessing Your Creativity *by Rev. Thomas Ryan, CSP*
Learn to cultivate your creative spirit.
6 x 9, 160 pp, Quality PB, 978-1-59473-243-0 **$16.99**

**Technology & Spirituality:** How the Information Revolution Affects Our Spiritual Lives *by Stephen K. Spyker*
6 x 9, 176 pp, HC, 978-1-59473-218-8 **$19.99**

**Money and the Way of Wisdom:** Insights from the Book of Proverbs
*by Timothy J. Sandoval, PhD*
6 x 9, 192 pp, Quality PB, 978-1-59473-245-4 **$16.99**

**Creating a Spiritual Retirement:** A Guide to the Unseen Possibilities in Our Lives
*by Molly Srode* 6 x 9, 208 pp, b/w photos, Quality PB, 978-1-59473-050-4 **$14.99**
HC, 978-1-893361-75-1 **$19.95**

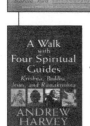

**Finding Hope:** Cultivating God's Gift of a Hopeful Spirit
*by Marcia Ford* 8 x 8, 200 pp, Quality PB, 978-1-59473-211-9 **$16.99**

**The Geography of Faith:** Underground Conversations on Religious, Political and Social Change *by Daniel Berrigan and Robert Coles* 6 x 9, 224 pp, Quality PB, 978-1-893361-40-9 **$16.95**

**Jewish Spirituality:** A Brief Introduction for Christians *by Lawrence Kushner*
5½ x 8½, 112 pp, Quality PB, 978-1-58023-150-3 **$12.95** *(A book from Jewish Lights, SkyLight Paths' sister imprint)*

**Journeys of Simplicity:** Traveling Light with Thomas Merton, Bashō, Edward Abbey, Annie Dillard & Others *by Philip Harnden*
5 x 7¼, 144 pp, Quality PB, 978-1-59473-181-5 **$12.99** 128 pp, HC, 978-1-893361-76-8 **$16.95**

**Keeping Spiritual Balance As We Grow Older:** More than 65 Creative Ways to Use Purpose, Prayer, and the Power of Spirit to Build a Meaningful Retirement
*by Molly and Bernie Srode* 8 x 8, 224 pp, Quality PB, 978-1-59473-042-9 **$16.99**

*Or phone, fax, mail or e-mail to:* SKYLIGHT PATHS Publishing
Sunset Farm Offices, Route 4 • P.O. Box 237 • Woodstock, Vermont 05091
Tel: (802) 457-4000 • Fax: (802) 457-4004 • www.skylightpaths.com
*Credit card orders:* (800) 962-4544 (8:30AM–5:30PM ET Monday–Friday)
*Generous discounts on quantity orders. SATISFACTION GUARANTEED. Prices subject to change.*

# Spiritual Practice

**Soul Fire:** Accessing Your Creativity *by Rev. Thomas Ryan, CSP*
Shows you how to cultivate your creative spirit as a way to encourage personal growth.
6 x 9, 160 pp, Quality PB, 978-1-59473-243-0 **$16.99**

**Running—The Sacred Art:** Preparing to Practice
*by Dr. Warren A. Kay; Foreword by Kristin Armstrong*
Examines how your daily run can enrich your spiritual life.
5½ x 8½, 160 pp, Quality PB, 978-1-59473-227-0 **$16.99**

**Hospitality—The Sacred Art:** Discovering the Hidden Spiritual Power
of Invitation and Welcome *by Rev. Nanette Sawyer; Foreword by Rev. Dirk Ficca*
Explores how this ancient spiritual practice can transform your relationships.
5½ x 8½, 192 pp, Quality PB, 978-1-59473-228-7 **$16.99**

**Thanking & Blessing—The Sacred Art:** Spiritual Vitality through
Gratefulness *by Jay Marshall, PhD; Foreword by Philip Gulley*
Offers practical tips for uncovering the blessed wonder in our lives—even in trying circumstances. 5½ x 8½, 176 pp, Quality PB, 978-1-59473-231-7 **$16.99**

**Everyday Herbs in Spiritual Life:** A Guide to Many Practices
*by Michael J. Caduto; Foreword by Rosemary Gladstar* Explores the power of herbs.
7 x 9, 208 pp, 21 b/w illustrations, Quality PB, 978-1-59473-174-7 **$16.99**

**Divining the Body:** Reclaim the Holiness of Your Physical Self *by Jan Phillips*
8 x 8, 256 pp, Quality PB, 978-1-59473-080-1 **$16.99**

**Finding Time for the Timeless:** Spirituality in the Workweek
*by John McQuiston II* Simple stories show you how refocus your daily life.
5½ x 6¼, 208 pp, HC, 978-1-59473-035-1 **$17.99**

**The Gospel of Thomas:** A Guidebook for Spiritual Practice
*by Ron Miller; Translations by Stevan Davies*
6 x 9, 160 pp, Quality PB, 978-1-59473-047-4 **$14.99**

**Earth, Water, Fire, and Air:** Essential Ways of Connecting to Spirit
*by Cait Johnson* 6 x 9, 224 pp, HC, 978-1-893361-65-2 **$19.95**

**Labyrinths from the Outside In:** Walking to Spiritual Insight—A Beginner's Guide
*by Donna Schaper and Carole Ann Camp*
6 x 9, 208 pp, b/w illus. and photos, Quality PB, 978-1-893361-18-8 **$16.95**

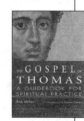

**Practicing the Sacred Art of Listening:** A Guide to Enrich Your Relationships
and Kindle Your Spiritual Life—The Listening Center Workshop
*by Kay Lindahl* 8 x 8, 176 pp, Quality PB, 978-1-893361-85-0 **$16.95**

**Releasing the Creative Spirit:** Unleash the Creativity in Your Life
*by Dan Wakefield* 7 x 10, 256 pp, Quality PB, 978-1-893361-36-2 **$16.95**

**The Sacred Art of Bowing:** Preparing to Practice
*by Andi Young* 5½ x 8½, 128 pp, b/w illus., Quality PB, 978-1-893361-82-9 **$14.95**

**The Sacred Art of Chant:** Preparing to Practice
*by Ana Hernández* 5½ x 8½, 192 pp, Quality PB, 978-1-59473-036-8 **$15.99**

**The Sacred Art of Fasting:** Preparing to Practice
*by Thomas Ryan, CSP* 5½ x 8½, 192 pp, Quality PB, 978-1-59473-078-8 **$15.99**

**The Sacred Art of Forgiveness:** Forgiving Ourselves and Others through God's Grace
*by Marcia Ford* 8 x 8, 176 pp, Quality PB, 978-1-59473-175-4 **$16.99**

**The Sacred Art of Listening:** Forty Reflections for Cultivating a Spiritual Practice
*by Kay Lindahl; Illustrations by Amy Schnapper*
8 x 8, 160 pp, b/w illus., Quality PB, 978-1-893361-44-7 **$16.99**

**The Sacred Art of Lovingkindness:** Preparing to Practice
*by Rabbi Rami Shapiro; Foreword by Marcia Ford* 5½ x 8½, 176 pp, Quality PB, 978-1-59473-151-8 **$16.99**

**Sacred Speech:** A Practical Guide for Keeping Spirit in Your Speech
*by Rev. Donna Schaper* 6 x 9, 176 pp, Quality PB, 978-1-59473-068-9 **$15.99**
HC, 978-1-893361-74-4 **$21.95**

# Sacred Texts—SkyLight Illuminations Series

Offers today's spiritual seeker an accessible entry into the great classic texts of the world's spiritual traditions. Each classic is presented in an accessible translation, with facing pages of guided commentary from experts, giving you the keys you need to understand the history, context and meaning of the text. This series enables you, whatever your background, to experience and understand classic spiritual texts directly, and to make them a part of your life.

## CHRISTIANITY

**The End of Days:** Essential Selections from Apocalyptic Texts— Annotated & Explained *Annotation by Robert G. Clouse*
Helps you understand the complex Christian visions of the end of the world.
5½ x 8½, 224 pp, Quality PB, 978-1-59473-170-9 **$16.99**

**The Hidden Gospel of Matthew:** Annotated & Explained
*Translation & Annotation by Ron Miller*
Takes you deep into the text cherished around the world to discover the words and events that have the strongest connection to the historical Jesus.
5½ x 8½, 272 pp, Quality PB, 978-1-59473-038-2 **$16.99**

**The Lost Sayings of Jesus:** Teachings from Ancient Christian, Jewish, Gnostic and Islamic Sources—Annotated & Explained
*Translation & Annotation by Andrew Phillip Smith; Foreword by Stephan A. Hoeller*
This collection of more than three hundred sayings depicts Jesus as a Wisdom teacher who speaks to people of all faiths as a mystic and spiritual master.
5½ x 8½, 240 pp, Quality PB, 978-1-59473-172-3 **$16.99**

**Philokalia:** The Eastern Christian Spiritual Texts—Selections Annotated & Explained *Annotation by Allyne Smith; Translation by G. E. H. Palmer, Phillip Sherrard and Bishop Kallistos Ware*
The first approachable introduction to the wisdom of the Philokalia, which is the classic text of Eastern Christian spirituality.
5½ x 8½, 240 pp, Quality PB, 978-1-59473-103-7 **$16.99**

**The Sacred Writings of Paul:** Selections Annotated & Explained
*Translation & Annotation by Ron Miller*
Explores the apostle Paul's core message of spiritual equality, freedom and joy.
5½ x 8½, 224 pp, Quality PB, 978-1-59473-213-3 **$16.99**

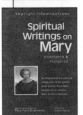

**Sex Texts from the Bible:** Selections Annotated & Explained
*Translation & Annotation by Teresa J. Hornsby; Foreword by Amy-Jill Levine*
Offers surprising insight into our modern sexual lives.
5½ x 8½, 208 pp, Quality PB, 978-1-59473-217-1 **$16.99**

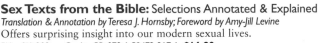

**Spiritual Writings on Mary:** Annotated & Explained
*Annotation by Mary Ford-Grabowsky; Foreword by Andrew Harvey*
Examines the role of Mary, the mother of Jesus, as a source of inspiration in history and in life today. 5½ x 8½, 288 pp, Quality PB, 978-1-59473-001-6 **$16.99**

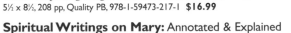

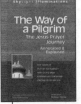

**The Way of a Pilgrim:** The Jesus Prayer Journey—Annotated & Explained
*Translation & Annotation by Gleb Pokrovsky; Foreword by Andrew Harvey*
This classic of Russian spirituality is the delightful account of one man who sets out to learn the prayer of the heart, also known as the "Jesus prayer."
5½ x 8½, 160 pp, Illus., Quality PB, 978-1-893361-31-7 **$14.95**

# Sacred Texts—cont.

## MORMONISM

**The Book of Mormon:** Selections Annotated & Explained
*Annotation by Jana Riess; Foreword by Phyllis Tickle*
Explores the sacred epic that is cherished by more than twelve million members of the LDS church as the keystone of their faith.
5½ x 8½, 272 pp, Quality PB, 978-1-59473-076-4 **$16.99**

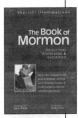

## NATIVE AMERICAN

**Native American Stories of the Sacred:** Annotated & Explained
*Retold & Annotated by Evan T. Pritchard*
Intended for more than entertainment, these teaching tales contain elegantly simple illustrations of time-honored truths.
5½ x 8½, 272 pp, Quality PB, 978-1-59473-112-9 **$16.99**

## GNOSTICISM

**Gnostic Writings on the Soul:** Annotated & Explained
*Translation & Annotation by Andrew Phillip Smith; Foreword by Stephan A. Hoeller*
Reveals the inspiring ways your soul can remember and return to its unique, divine purpose.
5½ x 8½, 144 pp, Quality PB, 978-1-59473-220-1 **$16.99**

**The Gospel of Philip:** Annotated & Explained
*Translation & Annotation by Andrew Phillip Smith; Foreword by Stevan Davies*
Reveals otherwise unrecorded sayings of Jesus and fragments of Gnostic mythology.
5½ x 8½, 160 pp, Quality PB, 978-1-59473-111-2 **$16.99**

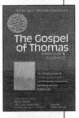

**The Gospel of Thomas:** Annotated & Explained
*Translation & Annotation by Stevan Davies* Sheds new light on the origins of Christianity and portrays Jesus as a wisdom-loving sage.
5½ x 8½, 192 pp, Quality PB, 978-1-893361-45-4 **$16.99**

**The Secret Book of John:** The Gnostic Gospel—Annotated & Explained
*Translation & Annotation by Stevan Davies* The most significant and influential text of the ancient Gnostic religion.
5½ x 8½, 208 pp, Quality PB, 978-1-59473-082-5 **$16.99**

## JUDAISM

**The Divine Feminine in Biblical Wisdom Literature**
Selections Annotated & Explained
*Translation & Annotation by Rabbi Rami Shapiro; Foreword by Rev. Cynthia Bourgeault, PhD*
Uses the Hebrew books of Psalms, Proverbs, Song of Songs, Ecclesiastes and Job, Wisdom literature and the Wisdom of Solomon to clarify who Wisdom is.
5½ x 8½, 240 pp, Quality PB, 978-1-59473-109-9 **$16.99**

**Ethics of the Sages:** *Pirke Avot*—Annotated & Explained
*Translation & Annotation by Rabbi Rami Shapiro* Clarifies the ethical teachings of the early Rabbis. 5½ x 8½, 192 pp, Quality PB, 978-1-59473-207-2 **$16.99**

**Hasidic Tales:** Annotated & Explained
*Translation & Annotation by Rabbi Rami Shapiro*
Introduces the legendary tales of the impassioned Hasidic rabbis, presenting them as stories rather than as parables. 5½ x 8½, 240 pp, Quality PB, 978-1-893361-86-7 **$16.95**

**The Hebrew Prophets:** Selections Annotated & Explained
*Translation & Annotation by Rabbi Rami Shapiro; Foreword by Zalman M. Schachter-Shalomi*
Focuses on the central themes covered by all the Hebrew prophets.
5½ x 8½, 224 pp, Quality PB, 978-1-59473-037-5 **$16.99**

**Zohar:** Annotated & Explained *Translation & Annotation by Daniel C. Matt*
The best-selling author of *The Essential Kabbalah* brings together in one place the most important teachings of the Zohar, the canonical text of Jewish mystical tradition.
5½ x 8½, 176 pp, Quality PB, 978-1-893361-51-5 **$15.99**

# Sacred Texts—cont.

## ISLAM

### The Qur'an and Sayings of Prophet Muhammad
Selections Annotated & Explained
*Annotation by Sohaib N. Sultan; Translation by Yusuf Ali; Revised by Sohaib N. Sultan*
*Foreword by Jane I. Smith*
Explores how the timeless wisdom of the Qur'an can enrich your own spiritual journey.
5½ x 8½, 256 pp, Quality PB, 978-1-59473-222-5 **$16.99**

### Rumi and Islam: Selections from His Stories, Poems, and Discourses—
Annotated & Explained
*Translation & Annotation by Ibrahim Gamard*
Focuses on Rumi's place within the Sufi tradition of Islam, providing insight into the mystical side of the religion.
5½ x 8½, 240 pp, Quality PB, 978-1-59473-002-3 **$15.99**

## EASTERN RELIGIONS

### The Art of War—Spirituality for Conflict
Annotated & Explained
*by Sun Tzu; Annotation by Thomas Huynh; Translation by Thomas Huynh and the Editors at Sonshi.com; Foreword by Marc Benioff; Preface by Thomas Cleary*
Highlights principles that encourage a perceptive and spiritual approach to conflict.
5½ x 8½, 256 pp, Quality PB, 978-1-59473-244-7 **$16.99**

### Bhagavad Gita: Annotated & Explained
*Translation by Shri Purohit Swami; Annotation by Kendra Crossen Burroughs*
Explains references and philosophical terms, shares the interpretations of famous spiritual leaders and scholars, and more.
5½ x 8½, 192 pp, Quality PB, 978-1-893361-28-7 **$16.95**

### Dhammapada: Annotated & Explained
*Translation by Max Müller and revised by Jack Maguire; Annotation by Jack Maguire*
Contains all of Buddhism's key teachings.
5½ x 8½, 160 pp, b/w photos, Quality PB, 978-1-893361-42-3 **$14.95**

### Selections from the Gospel of Sri Ramakrishna
Annotated & Explained
*Translation by Swami Nikhilananda; Annotation by Kendra Crossen Burroughs*
Introduces the fascinating world of the Indian mystic and the universal appeal of his message.
5½ x 8½, 240 pp, b/w photos, Quality PB, 978-1-893361-46-1 **$16.95**

### Tao Te Ching: Annotated & Explained
*Translation & Annotation by Derek Lin; Foreword by Lama Surya Das*
Introduces an Eastern classic in an accessible, poetic and completely original way.
5½ x 8½, 192 pp, Quality PB, 978-1-59473-204-1 **$16.99**

## STOICISM

### The Meditations of Marcus Aurelius
Selections Annotated & Explained
*Annotation by Russell McNeil, PhD; Translation by George Long; Revised by Russell McNeil, PhD*
Offers insightful and engaging commentary into the historical background of Stoicism.
5½ x 8½, 288 pp, Quality PB, 978-1-59473-236-2 **$16.99**

# Kabbalah / Enneagram
## (Books from Jewish Lights Publishing, SkyLight Paths' sister imprint)

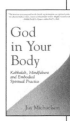

**God in Your Body:** Kabbalah, Mindfulness and Embodied Spiritual Practice
*by Jay Michaelson* 6 x 9, 288 pp, Quality PB Original, 978-1-58023-304-0 **$18.99**

**Cast in God's Image:** Discover Your Personality Type Using the Enneagram and Kabbalah
*by Rabbi Howard A. Addison* 7 x 9, 176 pp, Quality PB, 978-1-58023-124-4 **$16.95**

**Ehyeh:** A Kabbalah for Tomorrow *by Dr. Arthur Green*
6 x 9, 224 pp, Quality PB, 978-1-58023-213-5 **$16.99**

**The Enneagram and Kabbalah, 2nd Edition:** Reading Your Soul
*by Rabbi Howard A. Addison* 6 x 9, 192 pp, Quality PB, 978-1-58023-229-6 **$16.99**

**The Gift of Kabbalah:** Discovering the Secrets of Heaven, Renewing Your Life on Earth
*by Tamar Frankiel, PhD* 6 x 9, 256 pp, Quality PB, 978-1-58023-141-1 **$16.95**
HC, 978-1-58023-108-4 **$21.95**

**God and the Big Bang:** Discovering Harmony between Science and Spirituality
*by Dr. Daniel C. Matt* 6 x 9, 216 pp, Quality PB, 978-1-879045-89-7 **$16.99**

**Kabbalah:** A Brief Introduction for Christians
*by Tamar Frankiel, PhD* 5½ x 8½, 176 pp, Quality PB, 978-1-58023-303-3 **$16.99**

**Zohar:** Annotated & Explained *Translation and Annotation by Dr. Daniel C. Matt*
Foreword by Andrew Harvey 5½ x 8½, 176 pp, Quality PB, 978-1-893361-51-5 **$15.99**
*(A book from Jewish Lights, SkyLight Paths' sister imprint)*

# Judaism / Christianity / Interfaith

**Talking about God:** Exploring the Meaning of Religious Life with
Kierkegaard, Buber, Tillich and Heschel *by Daniel F. Polish, PhD*
Examines the meaning of the human religious experience with the greatest
theologians of modern times. 6 x 9, 176 pp, HC, 978-1-59473-230-0 **$21.99**

**The Jewish Approach to Repairing the World (*Tikkun Olam*)**
A Brief Introduction for Christians *by Rabbi Elliot N. Dorff, PhD, with Reverend Cory Willson*
A window into the Jewish idea of responsibility to care for the world.
5½ x 8½, 256 pp, Quality PB, 978-1-58023-349-1 **$16.99** *(A book from Jewish Lights, SkyLight Paths' sister imprint)*

**Modern Jews Engage the New Testament:** Enhancing Jewish Well-Being in a Christian Environment *by Rabbi Michael J. Cook, PhD*
A look at the dynamics of the New Testament. 6 x 9, 416 pp, HC, 978-1-58023-313-2 **$29.99**
*(A book from Jewish Lights, SkyLight Paths' sister imprint)*

**The Changing Christian World:** A Brief Introduction for Jews
*by Rabbi Leonard A. Schoolman* 5½ x 8½, 176 pp, Quality PB, 978-1-58023-344-6 **$16.99**
*(A book from Jewish Lights, SkyLight Paths' sister imprint)*

**The Jewish Connection to Israel, the Promised Land:** A Brief Introduction for
Christians *by Rabbi Eugene Korn, PhD* 5½ x 8½, 192 pp, Quality PB, 978-1-58023-318-7 **$14.99**
*(A book from Jewish Lights, SkyLight Paths' sister imprint)*

**The Jewish Approach to God:** A Brief Introduction for Christians *by Rabbi Neil Gillman*
5½ x 8½, 192 pp, Quality PB, 978-1-58023-190-9 **$16.95** *(A book from Jewish Lights, SkyLight Paths' sister imprint)*

**Jewish Ritual:** A Brief Introduction for Christians
*by Rabbi Kerry M. Olitzky and Rabbi Daniel Judson* 5½ x 8½, 144 pp, Quality PB, 978-1-58023-210-4 **$14.99**
*(A book from Jewish Lights, SkyLight Paths' sister imprint)*

**Jewish Spirituality:** A Brief Introduction for Christians *by Rabbi Lawrence Kushner*
5½ x 8½, 112 pp, Quality PB, 978-1-58023-150-3 **$12.95** *(A book from Jewish Lights, SkyLight Paths' sister imprint)*

# About SKYLIGHT PATHS Publishing

SkyLight Paths Publishing is creating a place where people of different spiritual traditions come together for challenge and inspiration, a place where we can help each other understand the mystery that lies at the heart of our existence.

Through spirituality, our religious beliefs are increasingly becoming a part of our lives—rather than *apart* from our lives. While many of us may be more interested than ever in spiritual growth, we may be less firmly planted in traditional religion. Yet, we do want to deepen our relationship to the sacred, to learn from our own as well as from other faith traditions, and to practice in new ways.

SkyLight Paths sees both believers and seekers as a community that increasingly transcends traditional boundaries of religion and denomination—people wanting to learn from each other, *walking together, finding the way.*

For your information and convenience, at the back of this book we have provided a list of other SkyLight Paths books you might find interesting and useful. They cover the following subjects:

| | | |
|---|---|---|
| Buddhism / Zen | Gnosticism | Mysticism |
| Catholicism | Hinduism / | Poetry |
| Children's Books | Vedanta | Prayer |
| Christianity | Inspiration | Religious Etiquette |
| Comparative | Islam / Sufism | Retirement |
| Religion | Judaism / Kabbalah / | Spiritual Biography |
| Current Events | Enneagram | Spiritual Direction |
| Earth-Based | Meditation | Spirituality |
| Spirituality | Midrash Fiction | Women's Interest |
| Global Spiritual | Monasticism | Worship |
| Perspectives | | |

*Or phone, fax, mail or e-mail to:* SKYLIGHT PATHS Publishing
Sunset Farm Offices, Route 4 • P.O. Box 237 • Woodstock, Vermont 05091
Tel: (802) 457-4000 • Fax: (802) 457-4004 • www.skylightpaths.com
**Credit card orders:** (800) 962-4544 (8:30AM–5:30PM ET Monday–Friday)
Generous discounts on quantity orders. SATISFACTION GUARANTEED. Prices subject to change.